Molly and Me

by

Marion Lewis Besmehn

To Joy!
Listening to you
I first became aware
of the true power of stories
over life. Thank you.
Marion Lewis Besmehn

PANGEA PUBLISHING
www.PangeaCorp.com

PUBLISHED BY

PANGEA

www.pangeacorp.com

ISBN: 978-0-9894065-1-2

Published by PANGEA www.pangeacorp.com

I started putting together family stories for my one granddaughter, Kristen. By the time I finished I had nine grandchildren and one great grandchild: Elias, Gabe, Ashley, Abby, Allie, Sam, Chase, Cole, and Gavin.

I have also come to think of my brother Billy's grandchildren as my own: Kristina and Courtney.

I hope all my family know how much I love them.

Marion Lewis Besmehn

MAPS

ACKNOWLEDGMENTS

Doug Lipman is a storyteller and a storytelling coach. He has written an epic mystical story, *The Soul of Hope*. In his story, he connects with his culture and his ancestors in their struggle to pass on from one generation to the next their most highly prized treasures, faith and hope. Doug tells this story through several lifetimes.

It may be presumptuous of me to think my story has any connection to his but I hope and pray it does.

My name is Marion Lewis Besmehn; I was born in Wales, in the small seaside town of Beaumaris, on the Isle of Anglesey, North Wales. I come from a cultural tradition of storytelling. How I loved listening to my grandmother and grandfather tell stories!

When I was fifty, I discovered the World of Storytelling in Jonesborough, Tennessee. I listened to stories by Jay O'Callahan, Ed Stivender, Doug Lipman, and many more. I studied Storytelling at East Tennessee State University in Johnson City, Tennessee. As late as it was for me and as impossible a challenge, I had the dream of becoming a professional storyteller! I was inspired by the best—Jay, Ed,

Doug and all the storytellers in Jonesborough, Tennessee.

Not as easy as it looks! These guys are fantastic! Up to the time I realized I wanted to be a storyteller, my proudest accomplishment had been to be a wife and mother of three grown sons.

I started learning the art of storytelling with zero confidence. Just standing up in front of an audience made me question my sanity. Still, ("God give me strength!") I pursued and am still pursuing storytelling.

Now, I am an old lady. Before it's too late —and with encouragement from Jay O'Callahan, Doug Lipman, and Doug's wife, Pam McGrath—I have written the story I thought I would never tell.

Doug Lipman said he'd coach me, and without his invaluable help I would never have been able to tell my truth.

FORWARD

The Dark Side of Story—and a Bright Hope

Story is powerful and can transform us. Yet not all stories transform us in ways that make us bigger.

Marion Besmehn's mother, Molly, possessed the power of story, but she used it to manipulate, to shape the world to her ever-changing whims. In the end, Molly was a prisoner of her own manipulation; as much as she used it to bend the wills of others to hers, her commitment to being the pitiable heroine of a tragedy drew her on (and isolated her) like an addictive drug.

So what are the odds that Marion, the child of such a mother, would be able to emerge whole?

Molly and Me tells us a story of a submissive child who, faced with her mother's overpowering abilities to distort the truth, finds a single path out of that darkness: to resist her mother's false truths and cling to her own. She escapes from her mother's critical pull, marries a good man, and raises a family. As long as Marion is occupied with the challenges of managing a family that moves 18 times in 30 years, her mother is little more than a painful annoyance. But once Marion's children are grown, Marion has to face the voice of her long dead mother that still lives in her own mind, telling her how dull, weak, and timid she is.

What Marion's skillful collection of interlocking stories shows us is that, when a significant human relationship, or even a life, can't have a happy ending, it's still possible to take control of our perceptions by shaping the story we tell ourselves about our life, by experiencing in story the things that life never gave us, and by transforming a traumatic story into a triumph—if not of happiness, then of wholeness.

With its honesty, humility, and surprising humor, *Molly and Me* leaves this storytelling coach feeling moved, buoyed and cleansed—and inspired to take charge of shaping my own life story into an honest and integrated whole.

Is there really anything more hopeful than that?

Doug Lipman
Story Dynamics

2010

PLANE TO NEW YORK

The flight attendant has just announced we are at the prescribed ten thousand feet. Okay, Marion, it's now or never. Turn the laptop around. Open the lid and push the tiny round thingamabob. Da-dumm! So far, so good.

A few minutes ago, as the plane was climbing out of San Francisco's persistent fog, I took from my wallet a small crumpled piece of paper I'd buried deep in my wallet twenty-four years ago—not this exact wallet, I've gone through several in the last twenty-four years. I just move the piece of paper along with my current driver's license and credit cards to the next wallet. I haven't actually looked at the words I wrote down in front of the statue of Mary, but the gist is tattooed on my brain and the knife is still stuck in my heart!

Well, okay, that's pretty melodramatic, but listen to what happens inside my head as I spell out M-O-L-L-Y on my new computer...

MISS HIGH AND MIGHTY'S GOING TO SPILL HER GUTS? DON'T MAKE ME LAUGH, YOU LITTLE BITCH; DO YOU HONESTLY THINK YOU CAN PUT YOUR MADE-UP STORIES IN THAT COMPUTER CONTRAPTION AND COME

OUT SMELLING LIKE A ROSE? NOTHING IS FURTHER FROM THE TRUTH!

There go my toes curling and my body temperature plunging colder than if Molly pushed me out the window at—what now? Twenty-thousand feet?

I stare at the small Post-It I stuck to the top of my screen before I left home: "Tell what I know to be the truth!"

Oh God, how will I ever get it down if I can't control her voice in my head and my body goes into overdrive? This is never going to work...

THAT'S THE POINT, STEW-PIT. I, YOUR MOTHER, AM THE ONLY ONE WHO KNOWS THE REAL TRUTH! YOU UNGRATEFUL HUSSY!

Mom, that's enough! With the help of this computer, I will get my side of the story down, so just put that in your pipe and smoke it!

Silence—blissful silence!

That's telling her. Too bad she's dead!

Suddenly, the good-looking older gentleman sitting across the aisle from me, reaches over, grabs both my hands off the computer and says, "Marry me?"

I'm dumbfounded. Our eyes meet; I laugh and say, "I did, fifty years ago!"

"Would you do it again?"

I squeeze his hands, "In a heartbeat!"

It's our anniversary. Fifty years! Unbelievable! We are on our way to New York to board the Queen Mary 2.

Yes, it's a trip of a lifetime to celebrate our marriage, but also, for the six days we're on the Queen Mary, Chuck and I have made a bargain. During the day while he's at the ship's gym exercising and then attending the lectures the ship offers, I am going to get Molly on my computer and out of my head once and for all!

YOU, MY CHILD, ARE OUT OF YOUR MIND! HOW MANY TIMES HAVE I TOLD YOU: YOU WILL NEVER BE RID OF ME, I AM YOUR MOTHER! MY VOICE IS THE TRUTH! YOU LITTLE BITCH, WAIT UNTIL YOU'RE DEAD. THEN YOU WILL SEE HOW RIGHT I AM!

Mom, I'm not going there... I mean, well, I hope not just yet. But before I do die, I am determined to straighten out exactly what happened and why I can't get rid of your voice inside my head!

Pong! Pong! Oh my God, the plane is dropping! I see the piece of paper from my wallet fly to the aisle between my husband and me! Chuck is reaching down...

"What's this? Important?" He's starting to straighten—I grab it out of his hands. He pulls his hands back and mouths, "Ouch!"

"Yes! No! That's okay, just notes to myself." Damn, I feel a tear sliding down my nose.

"Marion, Marion, Marion, are you absolutely sure you want to write about Molly while we're on vacation? I know you, Marion. You're going to conjure up all sorts of Catholic guilt—all because of your dear, sweet, saintly mother!"

"Very funny. Look—she's already broken my laptop!"

My husband gives me his incredulous look. "Let me see."

I hand over the black screen laptop.

"It's fine. Just hit the long black bar, the space bar—not the re-bar, as you call it."

The lady in the aisle seat ahead of Chuck turns around to look at us. I feel my face burning. I try to take back the laptop, but Chuck is typing. I lean over and read the screen as I wipe my nose with my sleeve.

Honey, this laptop is tough! You're tough! The witch is dead! Write what you want, but please, don't let her make you crazy! I'll back up what you want to save and remember you promised to stop writing every evening before dinner! We have reservations tonight in New York, and every night on the Queen Mary 2!

I take back the computer. Whoa! The plane takes a huge tumble. I hate, hate turbulence. I'm trying to center myself as I'm screaming inside my head—*Mom, I'm not scared of you! Just stop it!*

Great, just great! The minute I start thinking, writing one word about Molly, I'm back down the black hole I thought I climbed out of a long time ago. Holding down the rattling food tray that my laptop sits atop with one hand and the other clutching the retrieved unable-to-lose, unable to actually read, stupid piece of paper, I cram it back in my wallet. I shove the wallet back in the purse that's stuffed beside me in the *not* spacious airplane seat. All elbows, I'm invading space not assigned to me. Bending over the aisle to place the purse under the seat, I realize Houdini would have been faster and more graceful ridding himself of locked chains under water. Still holding down my computer, I kick the purse under the seat with my foot because there's no space to kick myself! Why the hell do I still have that piece of paper?

Marion, forget the paper! What will I put in this computer to make my mother stop screaming at me?

The plane rights itself but is continuing to shudder. I'm taking deep breaths and making myself concentrate on my trembling fingers.

Sticks and stones may break my bones, but words will never hurt me.

Where did that come from? I remember: I used to say that to myself all the time when I was little. God give me strength.

*Hell yes, I can, I **will**—do this!*

MARION, YOU ARE PATHETIC! YOU HAVE NO IDEA WHO YOU ARE DEALING WITH! YOU THINK YOU CAN MAKE EVERYTHING RIGHT WITH THAT SILLY TOY? DEAD OR ALIVE, THE TRUTH IS, I AM YOUR MOTHER, AND I AM THE ONLY ONE WHO KNOWS THE TRUTH! AND THE ULTIMATE TRUTH IS: YOU'RE GOING TO HELL!

Breathe, Marion, breathe!

Okay Mom, fasten your seat belt, turbulence or no turbulence, it's going to be a very bumpy ride. I'm going to get you out of my wallet, my gut, my head! I will put the truth, as I know it, down in this computer, if it's the last thing I do—so help me God!

I come from other people besides you, Mom. And my truth begins, long before I was born. So just put these stories in your pipe and smoke them!

Marion Lewis Besmehn

PART I

STORIES BEFORE I WAS BORN

Wales

Beaumaris

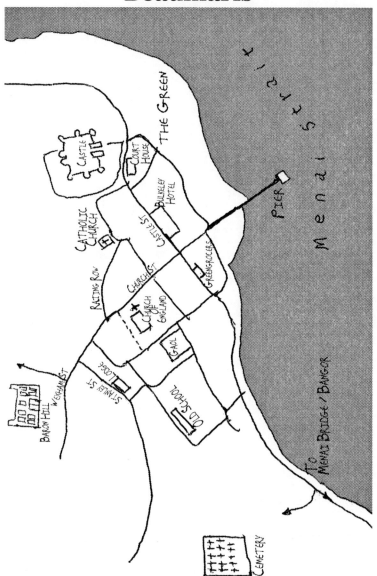

1900

THE COURTSHIP

"Miss Mary Anne McKeen?"

"Yes, that's right. I'm Mary Anne McKeen."

"I'm Will Lewis, Miss McKeen; I've been sent to fetch ye. Mrs. Pritchard, the cook at Baron Hill, says I'm to take ye to Mrs. Jones's where Father Brady's arranged a room for ye. Cook says to tell ye after you're settled in ye room, I'm to take ye up to Baron Hill so's ye can meet Mrs. Pritchard and get the lay of the land. She says to tell ye she's not expectin' ye to start work till Monday mornin'—half-past seven— sharp."

"I see. Thank ye for meeting me, Mr. Lewis. I thought perhaps Father Brady would be here."

"Aye, that he would, but Cook got a message from him early this morning. It seems old Mrs. Davis has taken a turn for the worse. She's got no family. He's hoping ya'd understand."

"Of course."

"Right, well come on then. Have I got all yer luggage?"

"Yes, that's it."

"Welcome to Beaumaris, Wales, Miss Mary Anne McKeen—from Ireland, isn't it."

"Yes—thank ye—ye're very kind."

Will couldn't help notice that Mary Anne was taller than most girls in the village. Tight curls sprang out from under and around the plain black hat she wore. But her eyes! Oh, her eyes: Will was completely taken aback by his feeling of falling head-over-heels into clear sparkling sky as she spoke to him.

About a fortnight (two weeks) after Will had brought Mary Anne to Baron Hill, he asked Cook if there was anything he could do for her.

"Aye, I don't suppose ye can carve a joint, can ye, Will?"

"Of course, I can carve a joint. Lead me to it, woman."

"No, no, not now, ye silly lout. I need someone for the 'do' Saturday night."

"What are ye babbling about woman? I'm a gardener, not a ruddy butler!"

"Aye, I know. It's just I'm in a terrible stew. Old Tom, who's carved the meat since before I come is laid up with rheumatism something terrible. I haven't the heart to ask him. That young Irish girl, Mary Anne, is going to serve. But the master will be awfully put out if I haven't a man carving the roast beef proper."

Will cut a dashing figure in his Sunday, go-to-meeting, blue suit, even though it was Saturday night. Mary Anne told him where to stand and how to put the thin slices of well done roast beef on each guest's plate. The two of them worked well together. Will was amazed with her efficiency and grace.

One afternoon, Cook, Mary Anne and Will were having tea in the kitchen. Will asked Mary Anne where exactly in Ireland did she come from? Mary Anne put her teacup back on the saucer and, after a long pause, replied "Athlone."

"I see in the paper that there was a bit of a skirmish at a fair outside Dublin. The I.R.B. says it means to make trouble for any and all British in the area."

"Aye, the Irish Republican Brotherhood is what they call themselves. They're a disgrace to Ireland and the Church. They're nothing but hoodlums bent on keeping Ireland in the Dark Ages."

Cook gave Mary Anne a fresh scone. "There, there, young lady, these are problems ye don't have to worry about. Let the men folk sort 'em out. Shame on ye, Will, for bringing up such a subject."

"Aye, Mrs. P., I'm sorry. But I like to hear what Mary Anne thinks. I wish I could take her to the pub and have the men hear what she has to say. They think all Irish Catholics want blood."

"Will, it doesn't matter what I think. I'm only a woman."

Will's teacup hit the saucer with a clang.

"Of course it matters what ye think. It's your country, isn't it? The troubles in Ireland will never end until people like ye are heard and believed. I admire ye, Mary Anne and I think ye right."

"Now, that'll be enough said cook. I'll not have my kitchen turned into a soapbox for politics. And have me dishes broken to boot."

Mary Anne stood up and said, as she took her dishes to the sink, "I'm sorry, Mrs. P. It was my fault. I spoke without thinking."

Will saw her turn from the sink. The pain in her eyes was inescapable. She said she would go and bring in some dried herbs from the garden shed. After she had left the room, Will looked at Cook. "What's going on? Did I miss something?"

"Will, I'm sorry. But ye're over yer head with this subject. It's best closed. I'll not say another word but ye'd better not be getting yer hopes up. She'll not be havin' anything to do with the likes of ye."

"Aye. Ye think she has a beau in Ireland?"

"Will Lewis! It's none of your business! Now go and dig up some potatoes for supper."

Will took his dishes to the sink, then got his coat from the peg. He went out into the garden before he realized he had no spade.

"Dear God, I can't think straight anymore."

He walked into the shed and surprised Mary Anne, who was standing with her back to him and crying softly.

"Mary Anne, what's wrong?"

"Will! Oh, it's nothing. I'm a little homesick!"

"Cook said I should have kept me mouth shut. I'm sorry—please forgive me. I wouldn't upset ye for the world."

"Ye didn't upset me. I did it meself. The truth of the matter is, what came out of me mouth back there in the kitchen is how I truly feel. But now that I've said it, I feel I've betrayed my country."

"Don't be daft, girl. Ye make more sense than all the bloody men in Ireland or Wales, for that matter. Did God put us on this earth to kill each other off? Say what ye think is right."

"Oh Will, it's no good. I did say what I believed and they threw me out."

"Good, they don't deserve ye. Mary Anne, I had no intention of saying anything just yet, but I can't help meself. Would you consider letting me court ye? With the clear understanding ye don't have to give me an answer right away."

"An answer? Do ye mean ye want to marry me? Dear God, ye can't be serious!"

"I am! I've never been more serious in me life. I know I'm not a Catholic, but I'll do whatever you want. I'll talk to Father Brady."

"I can't believe it! Will, ye know nothing about me. Oh God, I can't believe this happening. Please, I've got to go inside!"

She ran out of the shed and in the back door of the manor house. She turned into the small room the servants used as a parlor. As she entered the room, her legs suddenly gave from under her and she collapsed. Will was right behind her. He ran to her and picked her up in his arms.

"My God! What have I done?"

He carried her over to the settee.

"Mary Anne, it's all right. It's all right. Ye don't have to marry me. I'm so sorry. This is all me fault. Please, please forgive me."

Slowly, she opened her eyes.

"It's going to be all right, Mary Anne. Don't worry. I was a blithering idiot to have said what I did. I beg ye to forgive me!"

"Will, ye don't understand. It's not you—it's, it's me! Oh Will, ye need to talk to Father Brady. Tell him...tell him...I...I...said to tell ye why I can't marry ye. I can say no more. I need to go home."

"Ye want to go home to Ireland?"

"No, I can never go back to Ireland. I need to go to my room at Mrs. Jones. Would ya tell Cook I'm not feeling well and I'll be here a half hour early tomorrow?"

"I'll walk with ye and see ye get home all right."

"No, Will, I need to go alone. Thank you."

"Right. Mary Anne, wait here while I ask Cook if it's all right for ye to go. I think she said she wanted ye."

"Aye."

He walked out of the room. Cook was waiting for him in the kitchen.

"Right, where's me spuds?"

"Cook, can I have a word with ye, serious? I'm afraid I've gone and put me foot in me mouth."

"Aye, Will, what's the trouble?"

"It's Mary Anne. I didn't listen to ye and I blurted out asking her if I could court her? I'm afraid I've upset her something terrible. I don't think she should be alone tonight. Do ye think she could stay here with ye?"

"Oh, Will, is it that bad, is it?"

"Aye, something's terrible wrong. I think she needs another woman to talk to. Ye, me, Father Brady are the only friends she seems to have in the whole world."

"I'll go to her. Where is she?"

"She's in the servants' parlor."

"Right."

He puttered around the garden until after 6:00 o'clock. No one came out the back door, so he knew Cook had persuaded her to stay. He walked home with a heavy heart. The next morning, he was at Baron Hill before dawn. "Is she all right?"

"Aye, she's all right for the moment. But I'll tell ye this: Now that I know the whole story, that poor child has had an awful bad time."

"My God, why has her family abandoned her? Did she murder someone?"

"I'll not say another word. She wants ye to talk to Father Brady."

"Is she coming down?"

"No. I want ye to run down and ask the doctor if he can stop by some time today. I've given her strict orders to stay in bed."

"Right. Well, I'll go and see if I can get the doctor to come up and if ye haven't anything too pressing, I'll go and see Father Brady for a minute."

"Aye, that's a good lad."

Will got on his bike and fairly flew down Red Hill to the village. Will asked if the doctor would have a chance to go up to Baron Hill as Cook had requested he come. Then he jumped on his bike and went directly to the rectory of the little Catholic Church. The widow O'Brian, Father Brady's housekeeper, answered the door.

"Good-day, Mrs. O'Brian. Is Father Brady in? I'd like a word with him, if I might."

"Aye, he's in his study. It's William Lewis, isn't it?"

"Yes, that's right."

The widow O'Brian showed Will into a tiny parlor and left him. Will stood with his cap in his hand. After a few moments Father Brady walked into the parlor.

"William Lewis, is it?"

"Oh, yes, Father. I'm Will Lewis. I work up at Baron Hill."

"Yes, that's right. What can I do for ye, young man?"

"Father, I'll not beat about the bush. I want to court Mary Anne McKeen. But something's terrible wrong. She says I'm to come to ye and you'll tell me why I can't marry her. I'm a God-fearing man, Father, and I'm willin' to take instruction."

"I see. Tell me what's going on with the two of ye?"

"Father, ever since Mary Anne's come to Baron Hill, Mrs. Pritchard and me, why we've been like different people. She's a wonderful girl, Father. She's got a good head on her shoulders. Mrs. P. says she's got more brains than most girls put together. I know Mrs. Pritchard has come to think of her as the daughter she never had—and me, Father, I come to love her. I know something's happened in Ireland before she come and that's why she's here. Father, I need ye to tell me what happened, but I want ye to know...I love her."

"Aye son, I see, I see; well then, ye better sit down."

Will sat down on the small settee in front of the fireplace. Father struck a match and picked up a pipe laying on the small round table across from the settee. He sat in a shabby leather chair facing Will. As he puffed on his pipe, Will could feel the priest's reluctance to speak.

"You're sure Mary Anne told ye to come to me?"

"Aye, Father, she did."

"Right, well then I suppose there's nothing to do but give it to ye straight. Mind ye, young man, what I tell ye is not to go beyond these four walls. Do ye understand?"

"Father, I give ye me word."

"Well then, Mary Anne comes from the same town in Ireland as I do, Athlone. Up until a year and a half ago, she lived with her mother and stepfather. Her own father was killed when she was three years old. When she finished school, almost two years ago, she had wanted to go to a small college in Dublin, but her stepfather said absolutely no. She was very keen on studying Irish history.

Her parents were horrified and sent her to live with her maternal grandmother on the family farm about 15 miles outside Athlone. The old lady had two middle-aged sons running the farm. They had never married. It turns out Mary Anne's uncles were very much involved with the Irish Republican Brotherhood. Mary Anne said it took her a few days to realize what was going on. The men had a meeting at the farm, but the women were kept in the kitchen to provide food and drink. They were forbidden to listen to any of the meeting. A few days later, at the fair in Athlone, a British soldier was killed, and two civilians badly wounded.

"There was another meeting at the farmhouse the day after the incident; the men were congratulating themselves on a job well done. Mary Anne couldn't believe her ears. She had no idea her uncles were involved. It was against everything she believed in. She burst into their meeting and screamed that they were murderers and liars and that they had no idea what the word Christian meant.

"About that time one of her uncles hit her hard across the face. She lost consciousness. When she come to her senses, she was locked in her bedroom. She had no idea what time it was, but it was dark outside and the house was quiet. She slipped off the bed and opened the window. She climbed out of the window with the intention of getting away from the house and back to her mother. She says she remembers she was about a quarter of a mile from the house when someone attacked her from behind.

"She was found the next day in a ditch about two miles from the farm. She was barely alive. She had been beaten; and she had been... molested!

"She was brought back to her grandmother's house. Her grandmother took care of her, but told her it was all her own fault and that she had no right to say what she did and she had no business running away from the house in the middle of the night.

"Her uncles never came near her again. Her grandmother never reported the incident, telling Mary Anne it would be a terrible scandal for the family. Mary Anne's mother wasn't told until it became evident there was going to be a baby!"

"Good God!"

"The uncles arranged everything through her grandmother. The baby was to be taken by Mary Anne's parents. Mary Anne was to leave Ireland and not contact her family again. If she did not do exactly as she was told, her family would be in great jeopardy. The priest in Athlone was contacted and he got in touch with me. He does not know the whole truth.

"The first week she was here I knew she was carrying a heavy burden. I encouraged her to talk to me and she did. After she spoke to me I knew she felt a sense of relief. But I know she still feels a tremendous amount of anger besides the shame and guilt. Her life has been ruined and she has no one to turn to."

"I had no idea. Those bastards! How can they get away with it?"

"Aye, Will, there's much injustice in the world and women are the best target for men's hopelessness."

"Father, this just makes me want to marry her all the more. She needs me. I won't let her life be ruined by those bastards. God, if she'll have me I'll do everything I can to make it right for her."

"Will, ye're a good man. But ye have to realize a woman doesn't go through a terrible experience like this and come through without scars. Her mind may very well be affected and she may not want ye to...well...come near her."

"Aye, I know. But she's a strong girl. I won't accept her life being ruined by something she had no say in. If she'll have me, I promise with all my heart to do right by her as long as I live. Father, Father Brady do ye think you can convince her?"

"Me? Oh now, listen me boy, I'm just a priest! What in God's name do ye expect me to do?"

Sunday morning, Mary Anne felt well enough to go to Mass. Mrs. Pritchard said she would very much like to accompany Mary Anne to church. The two of them sat in the very back. When Mass was over, Father read a few announcements and then the banns of marriage.

"And now for the banns of marriage. I'm announcing for the first time, the intention of William Lewis from Beaumaris, Anglesey, and Miss Mary Ann McKeen from Athlone, Ireland."

Mary Anne sat motionless. As people left the church Mrs. Pritchard had to remind her church was over and would Mary Anne like to have a word with Father? By the time Mary Anne reached the rectory her Irish temper had set in. She pounded on the rectory door. Father was just buttoning the last button on his cassock as he flung the door open.

"Father Brady, who in God's name told ye to read the banns of marriage for Will Lewis and meself?"

"Come in, Mary Anne, Mrs. Pritchard, come in."

"Father, answer me question."

"Now, Mary Anne, please come in and we'll talk about it in a civilized manner."

Mrs. Pritchard pushed Mary Anne gently from behind. The two women walked through the doorway. Father ushered them in to the parlor. The gateleg table by the window was set with a white linen tablecloth and daffodils. There was a pound cake and trifle elegantly placed on glass plates. Will brought the teapot in as Father asked the ladies to be seated.

"I don't believe this! What on Earth's going on?"

Mrs. Pritchard spoke up. "Mary Anne, don't be angry. We just want ye to have a cup of tea and talk about the advantages of marrying Will Lewis."

"Mrs. Pritchard! What have you got to do with this?"

Father Brady interrupted, guiding her to the leather chair.

"Mary Anne, I know we took drastic measures and we're sorry. But we just want to present our case. Now, if after ye've heard us out and ye've a different mind, we'll abide by it. Now, sit down and hear us out."

Mary Anne sat down.

"This is ridiculous!"

Will poured the tea and handed it to her.

"Aye, we know. Here, have a cup of tea."

Father Brady walked to the fireplace and turned around.

"Now, Miss McKeen, we've gathered here today under unusual circumstances. It seems Will Lewis has very serious intentions towards ye, but ye won't give the poor lad a chance. Now, Mrs. Pritchard and meself, being a bit older and wiser than ye, have decided to take matters into our own hands and give ye the benefit of our advice. He's a good man. And speaking as a priest, I think ye should give the matter serious thought. Mrs. Pritchard here has known him several years and has worked with him. She vouches that he's a hard worker, sober, sensible, and saves his money."

Mrs. P. broke in.

"Aye, love, and if he gives ye any problem at all, ye just tell me and I'll box his ears!"

Mary Anne sat dumbfounded. Will watched her. Her tea sat untouched on her knee; she closed her eyes. His heart sank as the seconds ticked away. Finally she opened her eyes; she deliberately picked up her tea cup and took a sip of tea, then she slowly put the cup back on the saucer. Again several moments passed, at long last she looked up and with her eyes twinkling she spoke, "I think ye Welsh are all...all...BLOODY DAFT!"

Then her sky blue eyes found Will's and she whispered, "Aye, Will, I'll think about it!"

1902

CHANGE OF HEART

Ellen Lewis spoke English well enough, but Welsh expressed her true feelings. In 1902, Ellen was an old lady of forty-eight. She had lived on the Island of Anglesey, in North Wales all her life. Ellen had been born on a farm near the market town of Llangefni, near the center of the Island. She and her husband John had come to the seaside town of Beaumaris, before their children had been born.

Will, her oldest, was now twenty-one and had just married an Irish Catholic girl, Mary Anne. Night after night, John listened as Ellen told him, in Welsh, exactly how she felt about a twenty-four year old Catholic girl that couldn't speak a word of Welsh, marrying her first born.

"Dydw i ddim yn ei hoffi. Mae hi'n rhy hen!" ("I don't like it. She's too old!")

The young couple had been married a little more than a month when Ellen finally relented and decided to pay her new daughter-in-law a visit.

Will and Mary Anne had let a cottage at the bottom of the hill in Rating Row, across the street from the Beaumaris castle. Ellen decided she would bring the newlyweds a wedding present. So on a chilly September afternoon, Ellen packed in her basket two loaves of unbaked bread dough. One loaf would be the present and one loaf was expected to be given back after they had risen by the fire and had been taken to Mr. Roberts, the baker, to be baked in the only oven in the town.

John and Ellen Lewis lived at 36 Wexham Street, half way up Red Hill, so it was all downhill to her son's cottage. Even so, by the time Ellen arrived at the cottage she was anticipating with great relish ridding herself of the heavy basket, plunking herself down in her son's chair by the fire, and drinking a cup of fresh brewed tea. It would be good to be made a fuss over by her new, foreign, over-the-hill daughter-in-law. As she unlatched the front gate of the tiny cottage and trudged up the last few steps, she felt old and tired—but suddenly a little excited. She knocked on the cottage door. No answer. She knocked louder. Still no answer. She opened the door, stuck her head in and shouted, "Yo hoo, yo hoo? Sut dach chi heddiw?"

The only sound Ellen could hear was the ticking of the small clock on the mantle. She entered the cottage and walked past the clock and into the tiny kitchen, thinking, *This is not right; where is she? Something's happened!* The moment she entered the kitchen, all her suspicions were confirmed.

"Dim tân!" ("No fire!")

Her heart sank to her shoes. To have no fire in the grate this late in the afternoon was unthinkable. Then her eyes caught the large piece of paper propped up on the kitchen table. "My God, Father," she said out loud. The English words just tumbled out of her mouth, frightening her almost as much as the piece of paper. She snatched the note up as if she were reading it. Of course she could not. It was written in English. As a matter of fact, if the note had been in Welsh, Ellen could still not have read it. Ellen had never been taught to read or write. But she was as sure as she knew her own name what the words said. Ellen felt sick to her stomach. She knew as sure as she knew her son Will, that this note would break his heart. An overwhelming feeling of regret and loss flooded over Ellen and tears as surprising as the English words dropped on the white paper, blurring the ink. She folded the wet note up and tucked it inside her blouse and picked up her basket. Still in a daze, she walked back toward the front door.

All the way up the hill, Ellen's only thought was of her son, Will, and how she would break the news to him that his wife had left him.

By the time she reached her cottage she had formed a plan. She would send Owen, her youngest, up to Baron Hill where Will was working and fetch him home. His real home. She would not let him go to that cottage and find it cold and empty as she had.

Will Lewis was working with a crew of men deep in the woods of Baron Hill. After his marriage he had been promoted to work in the Estate Forest. After her marriage, Mary Anne was no longer allowed to work in the manor house, as now her job was to take care of their home and her husband.

That morning, Will had told Mary Anne, his wife, he would not be home for dinner at midday because of where he was working. So Owen couldn't find his brother. He knew if he went home without Will his mother would only send him back out again. So Owen played with the dogs and threw stones in the pond, knowing his oldest brother would eventually turn up.

Will and the other men finally came down the path at 5 o'clock in the evening. The men were very tired, very hungry, and very dirty. Will was surprised to see his little brother waiting for him. Owen told Will he was to come home with him as their mam was in a proper tizzy. Will asked Owen, "Is Dad all right?"

"Aye, he was working in the back garden, fine as a fiddle, when I come to fetch ye."

In the meantime, Will's mother had been home all afternoon waiting for Will to turn up. She had scoured the cottage from top to bottom to keep her mind from dwelling on the good-for-nothing hussy who had left her son high and dry. At a quarter past four, Ellen Lewis was on her hands and knees scrubbing the kitchen floor for the third time. As she bent over the bucket to ring the floor rag out, suddenly all the pent up emotion of Ellen Lewis spewed out. She fell forward, barely catching herself on the bucket's rim. Tears sloshed into the dirty water. Huge sobs were finally let loose as she bent her head over the tin bucket. There, kneeling on the floor, hanging on to the bucket for dear life, Ellen cried her heart out. But she was not crying for her son or his runaway bride. She was, at last, crying for herself—and, if truth be known, she was crying for her own mother.

Ellen Parry had been married at sixteen to a farmer's son, five miles from her parent's farm in Llangefni. She was married on a Saturday. On the following Tuesday she had packed her bag and run the five miles back to her mother. Her mother had caught a glimpse of her daughter coming up the path carrying her suitcase from the upstairs window. Her mother had opened the window and yelled down.

"What in God's name are ye doing back? Ye'll not cross this doorstep. Ye're a married woman—turn yourself right around and get back to yer husband before he comes looking for ye with a strap!"

These words were the last her mother ever spoke to her. A week later her mother died of a massive stroke. Ellen did not cry when she heard of her mother's death, and she would not go to her mother's funeral. But, now, thirty years later, she was crying. Her mother had gone to her grave never knowing why her daughter had come home that day.

When Ellen had thrown a torn dress in her suitcase to go back to her mother, it wasn't the young husband she was running from: It was her father-in-law. He was a small but powerful man and he ruled the roost. The family lived in mortal fear.

Tuesday morning after her wedding, Ellen knew mortal fear. She thought she was alone in the house. The others were doing the farm chores. Ellen's job was to air the beds and sweep the upstairs.

He caught her in his and the mother's bedroom. At first she thought he was acting the fool. But she soon realized he was dead serious. He grabbed her, kissed her, and when she screamed and tried to push him away, he smacked her hard across the face and tore her dress. He threw her onto the bed. Twisting her arm behind her back, he whispered in her ear that he would kill her if she didn't shut up and stop fighting.

The only thing that saved Ellen was the bang of the front door and feet running up the stairs. He was furious at the interruption, but he let her go. She ran out of the master bedroom. Her mother-in-law, Elizabeth, was standing on the landing; she had a shotgun in her hand.

Ellen ran to the bedroom that was hers and her new husband's. She took off the torn frock and threw it in her suitcase. She put on her coat, grabbed the suitcase, ran down the stairs and out the front door.

She heard the gun just as her feet touched the gravel path.

When her mother turned her away, she didn't know what to do. Her husband found her wandering along the road, still in shock. He took her suitcase and put his arm around her. He didn't say a word.

When they got in sight of the farmhouse, Ellen stopped walking. She refused to move. Nothing would persuade her to go back into the house until her husband, John, finally spoke, saying his father was dead. He told her matter-of-factly she wasn't to worry, everything was going to be all right. And it was. He took her in the back door of the farmhouse. Elizabeth gave her a cup of tea and told John to fetch a blanket to put over his wife's shoulders.

The doctor was summoned. Elizabeth explained that her husband was cleaning his gun and it must have accidentally gone off. The doctor signed the death certificate and Ellen's father-in-law of four days was buried in a field furthest from the house. No mention was made of the circumstances of the father's death again.

Six days later, Ellen was told of her own mother's death.

The family continued to work the farm and live in the stone farmhouse. Elizabeth carried on taking care of the family with great devotion, but there was a dark emptiness in her the family couldn't or wouldn't try to approach. When Elizabeth died, Ellen was twenty-six. Her husband, John, came to her and said he could no longer bear to stay on at the farm. They sold their share of the farm and bought a house in Beaumaris. Their son, Will, was born less than a year later.

Now, kneeling over the bucket, Ellen felt her anger, her shame, her loss, buried so deep, so long ago, come spewing out as if it were moments since her father-in-law had attacked her, and her own mother had rejected her. Ellen put her head down; kneeling on the floor, she sobbed, "Oh Mam, rwyf wrth fy modd i chi, yr wyf yn dy garu di." ("Oh, Mom, I love you, I love you.")

This is how Will and Owen found their mother when they walked in the back door. Will couldn't get a coherent word out of her. Finally it dawned on him: this all had something to do with his wife, Mary Anne. He shot out of the house and down the hill to his own cottage. His mother begged him not to leave, but when he did she followed him out the door and down the hill. Owen couldn't make head nor tail of what was going on, so he was right behind his mother. Ellen's husband, John, had been working in the garden all afternoon. He had been aware of the comings and goings of his family. Looking at his pocket watch (a quarter to six), he knew there would be no supper on the table. He decided he might just as well see what all the uproar was about. He lit a pipe and set off down the hill after his family.

In Bangor, eight miles away on the mainland, Mary Anne, Will's wife of six weeks, had caught the half-past-four carriage back to Beaumaris. She was with her friend, Annie Hogan, newly arrived from Ireland. Mary Anne and Annie had had a wonderful day in Bangor, shopping for material for Annie's wedding dress.

Unfortunately, the carriage lost a wheel and broke down just after the bridge. They had to walk the last five miles back to Beaumaris. Both girls were in high spirits, despite having to walk.

Mary Anne realized Will would be home before her, but she had left the note for him and dinner would be ready in a jiffy. Along with some very pretty pink taffeta material, both girls had purchased small tins of smoked ham. A great treat. They had also splurged on two loaves of bread from the bakery in Bangor. Everyone was talking of how much better the bread was than homemade. The girls laughed at how Mr. Roberts had to keep a record of everyone's bread and did he really give you back the same bread you brought him?

As Mary Anne said good-bye to Annie at the corner, she could see up the street that her father-in-law was opening her front gate. She waved, but he didn't see her. The minute Mary Anne walked in her front door, she could hear Will's voice, loud and very angry.

"Blast it woman, tell me exactly what happened and where the hell is me wife?"

Will's father and brother were standing just inside the front door. Both of them jumped quickly aside when they saw Mary Anne. Their expressions turned from surprise to glee. Both put their hands over their mouths to stifle any sound. Mary Anne walked straight back to the kitchen and, putting her grocery basket on the table said, "Will somebody in the name of God tell me what's goin' on in me own house?"

Will saw her, caught his breath, and collapsed in his chair by the fireplace.

"Where in the hell have ye been? Ye've had us all worried sick."

"I went to Bangor with Annie. I left a note. We caught a carriage home, but it broke down and we had to walk from the bridge."

"Note? What note? Ye've no business going to Bangor. Where the bloody hell is me supper?"

Mrs. Ellen Lewis looked as if she were seeing a ghost. Suddenly she closed her eyes and held her hands together. As Mary Anne and Will were barking at each other, Ellen opened her eyes and brought out the folded piece of paper. She held it up and started speaking in Welsh. Mary Anne had no idea what her mother-in-law was saying, but she saw her note. She had had quite enough. Her Irish temper flared and she looked straight at Will and said, "Ye're filthy! Don't ye ever dare set foot in me kitchen in that state again. After ye've washed, you can fix yer own supper. It's in the basket. Please excuse me; I've had an exhausting day and I'm goin' to bed."

With that, she turned on her heels and left the kitchen. She swept past her father-in-law and her brother-in-law without so much as a hello, good-bye, or kiss my bicycle. She ran up the stairs. They watched her with their mouths gaping. They saw her open the bedroom door and a heartbeat later, they heard her bloodcurdling scream.

Will jumped up so fast the chair beneath him crashed to the floor. In his haste he bumped into the kitchen table and the shopping basket contents went sprawling across the floor. He yelled as he ran, "Mary Anne, what's wrong?"

He took the stairs three at a time. At the top of the stairs, she was in his arms. Her whole body was trembling.

"Will, Will—someone's on our bed!"

The father and brother were right behind Will on the stairs. Will put Mary Anne behind him. He slowly opened the bedroom door and peered in. He could see someone was lying on top of the bed. He carefully closed the door and whispered to Mary Anne, "Don't be frightened. It's probably the old man next door. He's got the wrong house is all."

He opened the door again and all four tiptoed in, making a semicircle around the bed.

Owen stage-whispered, "Mary Anne, he didn't wake up when ye screamed—I'll wager he's kicked the bucket!"

Will still had his arm around Mary Anne. Her anger and fright melted away as she blessed herself: "Oh, dear God. May the souls of the departed rest in peace."

Will's mother walked into the bedroom. She put her hands straight into the air and started speaking in Welsh. Mary Anne whispered to Will, "I'll go and get the chapel minister."

Will whispered back, "Hold on, Mary Anne."

He kept his arm tight around his wife as his mother went on and on in Welsh. Owen and his dad were, by this time, at the head of the bed, one on either side. In a move that completely took Mary Anne's breath away, they stripped the extra eiderdown off the bed. Mary Anne gasped and hid her face in Will's shoulder. He squeezed her and bent down and whispered in her ear, "It's all right, Mary Anne, it's only several wadded up tea towels covering two loaves of bread!"

She peeked out from his shoulder and saw her mother-in-laws wadded tea towels along with several of her own tea towels spread out on top of the quilt that her best friend Annie had made for her wedding—and two loaves of well-protected, risen bread dough!

She looked up at Will and then over to her mother-in-law who was coming towards her. Mary Anne felt like screaming again, but she managed to stifle it. Ellen leaned over Will and took Mary Anne's face in her hands. In English she said, "Thank God ye come back to us. Ye're a good girl and young enough. I'm proud to have ye as me daughter-in-law. Now I'll not say another word. I'm going downstairs and fix us all a bit of supper. Ye two come down when ye're ready."

Ellen turned and on the way out of the bedroom spoke to her husband and young son.

"Ye two, make yourself useful and get that bread to the baker's before he shuts the shop. Be quick, I'll have supper on the table in two shakes of a lamb's tail."

Mary Anne and Will could hear the clatter of feet as everyone descended the stairs. At last they were alone. Mary Anne was the first to speak.

"Right, ye don't have to squeeze the living daylights out of me. I'm not goin' to run off. Although, I've a good mind..."

Will looked down at her and he could see a twinkle in her eye. He let her loose and spoke, "Mary Anne, I'm so sorry. Can ye forgive me? I had no right..."

"Will Lewis, it's yer mum who had no right. She took me note from the kitchen table; she thinks I'm too old for ye, and she put bread on our bed!"

They looked at each other and suddenly started to laugh. In a moment, they were in each other's arms, holding each other as they split their sides laughing.

Three quarters of an hour later, the family was sitting at the kitchen table, eating the tinned ham, boiled potatoes and carrots, and thick slices of the bakery bread from Bangor. Ellen looked up at her daughter-in-law and said, "Next week if ye have a minute, I'll show ye me own way of making bread. No sense ye having to go to the ends of the earth and wasting Will's hard earned money on store-bought bread."

Mary Anne and Will caught each other's eye just as they both were eating a piece of the bread in question. It was too late. Her eyes twinkled as she realized they had acquired a taste for bakery bread that very moment; but still she said, "That's very good of ye, Mother. Perhaps tomorrow ye'd drop by. I'll collect yer bread from Mr. Robert's and we'll have a slice or two with our tea."

"Aye, I'd like that, child."

Ellen never told Mary Anne the story of her father-in-law. But her husband, John, told his son Will, after Ellen died. When Will told Mary Anne, they both realized what suffering Will's mother had endured. After Mary Anne heard the whole story, she never let a day go by without saying a prayer for her mother-in-law, Ellen; she also remembered Elizabeth, Will's grandmother and Ellen's own mother.

1918

ON THE SLATE

Mary Anne opened the shop to the tinkling of the overhead bell. She had on her Sunday dress, her hat and her gloves. In her hands she clutched a gold chain attached to a small oblong purse. Mr. Jones, the greengrocer, looked up from behind the counter.

"Good afternoon, Mrs. Lewis. I've been expectin' ye. Come in, come in, can I get Mrs. Jones to bring ye a nice cup of tea?"

"Good afternoon, Mr. Jones. Certainly not! I'll not be drinking tea in the greengrocers."

"No, no, of course not. But I thought—well —I know how hard this is for ye and well, Mrs. Lewis, we all know it's a terrible mistake on the government's part and it will all be put right in the long run."

"Mr. Jones, what on earth do ye mean, 'we all know?'"

"Oh, Mrs. Lewis, Mrs. Owens, the postmistress, was in this mornin' and she told us—'it' didn't come."

"Dear God in heaven! Do you mean to tell me the whole town knows me business?"

"Now, now, Mrs. Lewis, these are trying times. There's a war on, the likes we've not known. We've got to stand together—help each other—if we've got any chance of beatin' these bloody Krauts."

"Mr. Jones, war or no war, I'll not have my business discussed behind me back at the greengrocers. Or anywhere else for that matter! Do I make myself perfectly clear?"

"Yes, yes, Mrs. Lewis, perfectly clear. I beg yer pardon. We—I—don't want to upset ye for the world!"

"I've a good mind to go to Mrs. Owens and give her a piece of my mind, I will!"

"Oh, now, Mrs. Lewis, she was only trying to help in her own way. She didn't mean any harm. Now what can I do for you?"

"Good God, give me strength. Well then, since ye *all* know—I have not received my husband's pay for over a month. Mr. Jones, I have four children to feed. I—I'm—obliged to ask ye if ye will allow me to run a bill for my groceries to feed the children until the war department deems fit to send me my husband's rightful pay. They've taken my children's father, and now they're taking the food right out of my children's mouths!"

"Mrs. Lewis, I would consider it an honor if ye'd let me put yer groceries on the slate. We all know—I mean, I know—this is all a terrible mistake on the government's part and it will all be put right shortly. Yer husband, Will, he'll be home soon and he'll have a word or two with the Army puttin' ye in this position."

"Aye, I never thought I'd see the day I'd have to beg for food for my children. But as sure as I'm standin' on this spot, I give ye me word, Mr. Jones, every penny will be paid back if I have to go back into service!"

"Mrs. Lewis, I'm not at all worried about the bill being paid. Now have ye got a list of what ye'll be wantin'?"

She opened her purse and drew out a small sheet of paper. She handed it to him and said, "This is very good of ye, Mr. Jones. I'll send the lads over after their lessons to collect 'em. Now, where do you want me to sign?"

"Mrs. Lewis, I trust ye! And I hope ye trust me. Go over what I can send ye this afternoon. If everything's correct, hold on to your bill and pay me when ye can. It's going to be all right. Ye'll see, Mrs. Lewis."

"Thank you, Mr. Jones. I'll write to my husband and tell him of your kindness. Good-day."

She turned to go—then turned back. She opened her purse and dug down coming up with a few coins. She put them on the countertop and said, "Mr. Jones, I think I have enough money for a tin of Black Cat cigarettes."

"Mrs. Lewis, I'm shocked! Don't tell me ye've taken up the filthy habit?"

"Mr. Jones, I beg your pardon. They're for my husband, Will. If ye must know, I'm puttin' a parcel in the post this afternoon."

"I know, I know, I was just pullin' ye leg! Here ye are then, a tin of Black Cat cigarettes. Oh, keep yer money. I'll just put em' on the slate."

"On the slate? Me bill? Oh no, Mr. Jones, you'll not be putting *cigarettes* on me bill! Now, I bought cigarettes for my husband, Will—and—I paid *cash* for them. Now you tell Mrs. Owens to put that in her pipe and smoke it! Thank you, Mr. Jones, and good-day to you."

She put the cigarettes along with two packages of digestive biscuits and a tin of sardines in the post to Will. Will had written not to send parcels as they took forever to reach him —if they weren't pinched. But she had to send him something from home, just as she had to pray for him morning, noon, and night. He was constantly in her thoughts and prayers as she went through the days, the weeks, the months.

Will, on the other hand, tried with all his heart not to think of her or the children. All around him men—boys really, hardly older than his sons—fell like flies. He knew it was just a question of time before it would be his turn. His only thought was, "Oh God, *please* make it stop. Make it *stop!*"

On October 2, 1918, he was climbing out of the trench when a German soldier surprised him. For a moment their eyes met. He was just a lad. Still the boy shot, and Will fell backwards—still clutching the ladder. Then he fell down, down into the French grave he'd always known was waiting for him.

On October 2, 1918, Mary Anne was at home washing the dishes. She pulled the stopper in the basin, and in the blink of an eye her wedding ring slipped off her finger and disappeared down the drain. Her heart skipped a beat and a prayer was on her lips. Something had happened to Will!

The weeks went by and there was no word. Then on November 11, 1918, the war was over. Still no word. Then on Christmas Day 1918, there was a knock on her front door. She opened the door and turned white as a sheet. For several moments she was incapable of uttering a sound. Finally she whispered, "Is it you? Is it really you?

"Aye, it's me. Didn't ye get a letter from the army tellin' ye I was being discharged?"

"Good God in heaven, I've had nought in the post from the army in four months!"

They stood looking at each other, both trying desperately to comprehend. Suddenly, tears streamed down her face and she said, "Oh Will, I was that sure ye were dead! I can't believe ye're standing in front of me. Thanks be to God, thanks be to God!"

She moved then and took him in her arms. As he put his arms around her and buried his face in her hair he said, "By rights, I should be dead." He reached into his pocket and drew out a battered cigarette tin.

"It was this that saved me! I got your parcel that very day. The note in the parcel said ye hoped I'd enjoy the sardines. But there were no sardines. The biscuits were smashed to smithereens. I took the cigarettes and slipped 'em in my left breast pocket. We were sent to the front right after that. Things were pretty quiet. But just as I was climbing out of the trench a German soldier appeared. The last thing I remember thinking—he's the spittin' image of our Johnny!"

Tears welled up in Will's eyes. She took the battered tin from his hand. She could see the small round hole that obliterated the head of the black cat. She opened the lid and inside the tin was the bullet. As she stood holding the tin with the bullet she began to realize what had been given back to her. Will was home, safe and sound. All her prayers had been answered. In one fleeting moment she knew the power of her prayers. But all she said was,

"Thank God I had enough money to pay for 'em!"

1920

WHISKEY

The clock on the mantle struck seven. The table had been set since five. She had long since taken the kettle off the fire. She looked once more out the window. Still no sign of him. She knew this could not go on much longer. But what could she do? Every time she tried to get to the bottom of what was wrong, he turned from her; and the more he turned from her, the more he turned to drink. Something had come between them. Something that was destroying him physically and mentally and breaking her heart.

When the clock struck eight and she found herself still sitting waiting for him, something inside her snapped. She stood up, walked to the sideboard, opened the bottom cupboard and took out the half bottle of whiskey. As she reached for a glass, she said out aloud, "I'm bloody well fed up! What's good for the gander is good for the goose!"

She poured the whiskey into the glass, then tipped the glass into her mouth. As the amber fire scorched a path down her throat, her whole body shuddered and she let go of the glass in her hand. It fell to the floor and smashed into bits, just as the door opened and Will walked in.

"What the bloody hell is going on in here?"

Tears filled her eyes as she struggled to gain control. She had taken much too big a gulp of the whiskey, and the effect was worsening. She fell back into the wooden chair. She could not speak. He came to her side, picking up the whiskey bottle as he passed the sideboard.

"How much of the bloody stuff did ye drink?"

Slowly the fire within her began to subside, but something else began to happen. Blood rushed to her cheeks and her eyes blazed. She sat perfectly still and riveted her eyes on him. Disgusted, he turned to put the whiskey bottle away. As he closed the cupboard, the full force of her anger hit him.

"I'm fed up, Will Lewis. I'll not put up with ye another day. I've let it go far too long as it is. Now, I'm puttin' me foot down. Ye won't tell me what's troubling ye, so ye're to go and ye're to speak to Father Brady!"

"What are ye blabberin' about, woman? I've got nothin' to say to a priest! Mind yer own business! I'll *not* go."

"Ye *will!* As God is me witness, if ye don't ye'll not come back in this house! Now, I'm layin' down the law. I'll not sit here day in and day out and watch ye kill yourself with drink!"

"Oh, and ye're a fine one to be talkin'. The kettle callin' the pot black, is it?"

There was a silence then. After a few moments she spoke.

"Will Lewis, ye know very well I don't drink. I took that whiskey to give me courage to say what I had to ye. Somethin's eating at ye and I can't be still and watch any longer. Now, ye'll do as ye're told or there will be bloody *hell* to pay. And I can promise ye that!"

"I'll not stay in me own house and listen to this rubbish!"

With that, he turned and walked out, slamming the door so hard the window panes rattled as if they'd break. She took a deep breath and immediately got the dustpan and brush. As she bent over sweeping up the broken bits of glass, she said, "Why in God's name did I drink that vile poison? Dear God, I promise ye, I'll not touch another drop to me lips, only please, please God, make Will go see Father!"

Father Brady had had a rotten day. It had been raining and he had discovered another leak in the church roof. He was sure he was coming down with the flu. He ate the cold supper that the widow O'Brian, his housekeeper, had put on the table before she left at three o'clock; he had said his prayers and climbed into bed. It was raining cats and dogs now and it irritated him no end to think of the water he'd have in the church tomorrow morning. He turned over, boxed the pillow, and pulled the eiderdown up to his ears. It made his blood run cold when he thought how tight his parishioners were when it came to money for church repairs. It was like asking brick walls!

"Aye, what will they do when the bricks come tumbling down? That'll show the blighters! It will be too late for 'em to sit up and take notice! Dear God, how can I get through to 'em before it's too late. Oh God, show me what ye want me to do with these bloomin' blighters!"

At midnight there was a terrific pounding on the presbytery door. As Father came to his senses, he could not distinguish the pounding of the door from the pounding in his head. He fumbled to light the candle by his bed. As he got to his feet and put on his dressing gown and slippers, he prayed to be forgiven for what he was about to say to the maniac breaking his door down. He lit the kerosene lamp in the hall and threw open the front door. Will Lewis was standing in the pouring rain, and Father let him have it.

"Good God, man, are ye trying to wake the dead? I've a good mind to send for the police for disturbin' the peace *and* destruction of property! Just look at the mark ye've put on me door! What in God's name do ye want, and have ye any idea what time it is?"

Will wore a silly grin as the water poured off his head and down his face. Not at all daunted by Father's upbraiding, he said, "I need to talk to ye, Father. I'm afraid I have had a few whiskies, and to tell ye the truth, I've no idea what time it is—as a matter of fact, I'm not at all sure I know what year it is!"

Father's temper rose to the boiling point as he realized he had been awakened by a drunk.

"Will Lewis, ye're *drunk*! Go home! And I hope yer wife boxes yer ears. Ye're a disgrace!"

Will's mood changed instantly. Suddenly he slumped forward, his right hand shot out to catch the doorjamb to steady himself.

"Right. I don't blame ye Father, ye're a good man. I have no business wakin' ye up in the middle of the night. Well, then. I'll trouble ye no more."

"For God's sake, Will, what's this all about? This is not like ye—has somethin' happened?"

"No, no, Father. Go back to bed—I'll not be troublin' ye no more."

Father reached out and grabbed Will's coat and pulled him inside the door—none too gently.

"Come in, ye old sot. Ye'll catch yer death and then there'll be hell to pay."

Father pulled Will to the leather chair in the parlor and pushed him down. Then he lit the ready fire (thank God for Mrs. O'Brian). As Father stood up and warmed his hands from the fresh flames, he turned. As he stared at the sorry heap in his one good chair he said, "I'd not be wanting to be in yer shoes, Will Lewis, when yer wife finds out ye've been traipsing around drunk all hours of the night! Now, get that wet coat off and tell me what this is all about."

Will fumbled with the brass buttons on his old army overcoat. As the warmth of the fire filled the small room the khaki coat gave off a strong, musty, wet wool smell. Will stood up, none too steady, and let his coat fall. Father caught the coat and put it over the straight back chair in the corner. Will took a couple of steps to the fire to warm himself. Father took a handkerchief from the pocket of his dressing gown and wiped the water off the leather chair that the coat had left behind. Will stood staring into the flames and spoke in a clear sober voice.

"Father, I don't think God believes in me any longer."

Father Brady finished wiping the chair, then draped the wet handkerchief over the fire guard.

"I see. Is this why ye woke me? And what in the name of God do ye want me to do about it in the middle of the night?"

Will sat back down in the leather chair, much to Father's annoyance. "Well, to tell ye the truth, ye can give me a drop of yer whiskey— seeing as now we're both wide awake."

"More whiskey, is it? What do ye take me for, a bloody fool? Ye're already three sheets to the wind! Stop the bloody nonsense and tell me what's on ye're mind before I send ye packin'."

"Ye're a hard man, Father. Well then, I'll come right out and tell ye. I've come to the end of me rope. I know it and Mary Anne knows it. I want ye to tell her for me that no man had a better wife. She didn't deserve the miserable husband she got. She and the children are the only reason I've hung on as long as I have."

"Will Lewis, for God's sake, that's the whiskey talkin'. Ye're not makin' any sense at all. If I didn't know ye any better, I'd swear ye were talkin' of doin' yerself in!"

"Aye, that I am, Father. And as God is my witness, it's not the whiskey talkin'. It's been two years comin' and if the truth be known, it's the whiskey that's kept me goin' as long as I have."

"Good God, man, ye can't be serious! What on earth led up to this?"

"Oh Father, it's all water under the bridge. The only thing I can't settle in me mind is Mary Anne and the children." Will was staring into the fire. A glazed look came into his eyes as if he were a thousand miles away.

For the first time Father was speechless, as it dawned on him the anguish and torment this man was feeling. Finally, Father said, "I think, perhaps, we *both* need a drink."

Father left the room and a few moments later returned with a full bottle of whiskey and two glasses. He set the bottle and glasses down on the small writing desk under the window. He unscrewed the cap of the whiskey bottle and poured two drinks. He handed one to Will and picked up the other for himself. Will took a huge gulp of the whiskey, leaned back in the chair, closed his eyes, and slowly began to speak.

"Have ye ever murdered anyone, Father? I have! Fair hair. Green eyes. Clean-shaven. So young."

Will took another drink without opening his eyes.

"The first few months when I got back from the war, I put it out of me mind. I was so relieved to be home—alive—with my wife and family. But slowly I began seeing his face when I closed me eyes. Then I started going over and over in me mind how it happened. Now I wake up thinking I'm the one who should be dead! I'm the one who should be *dead*!"

"So that's it, is it? How did it happen, Will?"

"How? Oh God, Father."

Will held his glass out and Father poured more whiskey. Will drained his glass before he spoke.

"We were on patrol and somehow I got separated from me company. I remember thinking I was bloody well lost, when the next thing I know there is a German soldier not five feet in front of me. We surprised the hell out of each other. I shot before I realized I pulled the trigger. The poor bugger was even more lost than me! It turned out there wasn't another Jerry within five miles of the area, and the gun he was carrying was worthless. Oh, God, he was only a lad, why did I kill him?"

Father took the desk chair and placed it in front of Will. He sat down and put his hands on Will's shoulders.

"Will, look at me."

Will opened his eyes.

"Now, nothing that I can say or do will bring that man's life back. But I can tell ye this: Ye have got to stop torturing yerself over his death. Ye did what ye had to do. Ye did what any one of us would have done under the same circumstances. Ye were in the middle of a war, Will! Now, thank God, that war is over. Ye have a wife and four children. What would they do without ye? Ye have got to get a grip on yerself. I'm telling ye yer time is not up yet and ye have responsibilities, my boy. Now, I'll not hear any more talk of doin' yerself in, do ye understand? I wish ye had come to me sooner, son. I had no idea what was going on in yer mind. But now that ye've come, we'll see this thing through."

Widow O'Brian arrived at the presbytery at six a.m. the following morning."Now, to fix a nice hot breakfast for Father after he says Mass."

As she turned the key in the lock of the back door of the presbytery, her mind was filled with her duties for the day. As she stepped into the kitchen, her nose was the first to detect something awry. There had been a fire in the fireplace, then damp musty wool enveloped her, and something else—yes, whiskey! Her ears were not nearly as efficient as her nose, so it took a moment for the terrible sound to register. But when it did, it frightened her beyond belief as she had no idea what it could be. She made the sign of the cross and said, "Mother of God, is it the devil's den I'm in?"

Just then there was a knock at the front door. Widow O'Brian's head was in a whirl. Never in her born days had she encountered anything like this. She backed out of the kitchen door and down the back steps, and as fast as her legs could carry her, she got herself to the front of the presbytery. She saw Mrs. Lewis standing at the front doorstep. She tried to call from the gate, but she was having trouble breathing. Just then Mary Anne turned and saw the housekeeper. She ran down the steps and put her arms around the old woman's shoulders, saying, "Mrs. O'Brian, what's wrong? There, there, now, it's all right. What's happened? Is it Father? He's not at the church."

"Oh, Mrs. Lewis, I don't know. There's terrible goings on in the house!"

"Where's Father? Have ye seen Father Brady?"

"No, no, I thought he was saying Mass. Somebody or something is in the house! We've got to get the police! Oh, they've murdered Father Brady in his bed! Mother of God, preserve us!"

"Now, now, Mrs. O'Brian, it's all right; show me."

"Oh, dear God, I'll not step in that house if me life depended on it!"

"All right, wait here. Is the back door open?"

"Aye, I left it gaping wide open!"

Mary Anne ran up the steps and in the back door. She moved quickly through the kitchen and into the parlor. Will was slumped in the leather chair by the fireplace. He was snoring to beat the band. She could not remember when she had seen him sleep so soundly. Father Brady was sitting at the small writing desk with his left cheek flat on the desk top. His right arm was stretched out. He must have hit the whiskey bottle when he moved his arm as it lay on its side, having dumped its contents down the side of the desk and into a huge sopping stain on the rug. The smell of whiskey was fierce. As Mary Anne stood staring at this unlikely scene, Father's eyes opened and he sat up.

"Mary Anne, ye're here!"

His hand rubbed his face and he mumbled, "I'm such a blithering idiot! God wants me to worry about the bloomin' blighters, not the bloomin' bricks!"

With this, his head fell back down on the desk and his eyes closed. Mary Anne turned and went back out the kitchen and down the steps to Mrs. O'Brian. Tears came to her eyes, but she was smiling and her heart cried, "Dear God, thank ye, thank ye."

The minute she saw Mrs. O'Brian, she began to laugh, "Mrs. O'Brian, it's all right, it's only my husband, Will and Father Brady. Believe it or not—they've both been doing exactly what they were told to do!"

 **1925**

THE BLACK DRESS

If you were in Beaumaris, on the Isle of Anglesey, North Wales, in the 1920's, the place to be after the sun went down was the music pavilion, way out on the pier. The local band was quite good and the family running the pavilion organized sing-alongs, taught dancing, and put on modest variety shows. The people on holiday from the mainland were fixtures at the music pavilion, but so were the local townspeople, especially the young people.

At the end of the summer of 1925, the music pavilion announced that there would be a ballroom dance contest. Two beautiful sterling silver cups, to be presented to the winners, were displayed.

This was the summer Molly Lewis turned seventeen and decided she would win one of those cups. Never mind that she was underage, did not have a partner, would never get permission from her Irish Catholic mother to be in a public dance competition, and, most importantly in her mind, did not have a proper costume. Still, Molly set her heart on winning the music pavilion's ballroom dance contest.

At the same time Molly found out about the dance contest, a very old and dear friend of Molly's mother died. Molly was very helpful in the kitchen, preparing food for after the funeral. Fixing a cup of tea for her mother, Molly said, "Mum, I won't go to the church service tomorrow. I'll stay here and be sure everything's ready for when everyone arrives."

"That's very sweet of ye, darlin', but I want ye at church with me. That's far more important."

"I know, Mum, but I don't have anything suitable to wear."

"Don't be silly. Ye can wear yer gray shirt and blouse."

"Oh Mum, I don't think that skirt fits anymore—and besides, I'm old enough, I should wear black to a funeral, especially this one. It's so important to ye."

"Yes, yes, darlin', ye're right. Perhaps I have something ye could wear."

"I think I saw a very suitable dress in the window of Pollycoff's in Bangor. Shall I catch the bus?"

The dress Molly wore to the funeral was black gabardine. It had a white lace collar and the skirt was long with two kick pleats starting at the bodice and continuing right down the front. The only thing interesting about the dress was it had a soft black sash instead of a belt. Molly's mother was very pleased, as it reminded her of a nun's habit, and she had never given up hope that Molly would contemplate the quiet life of a nun.

Molly's oldest brother, Johnny, had just turned twenty-two. He was very restless, ambitious, and he was in love. The young lady was not from Beaumaris, but she came every summer with her family for a holiday. This summer she had not yet made an appearance, but there had been much secret correspondence. Molly knew all about the letters and had threatened to tell, unless Johnny would go down to the music pavilion and sign up for the dance contest.

"Like bloody hell I will! I've got better things to do with me time than be in a stupid dance contest."

"Listen to me, John Lewis, if you think that highfalutin' girlfriend of yours will take any notice of a country bumpkin with no manners or no idea of the finer things in life, then you have got a rude awakening coming! You had better do as I tell you or you will have seen the last of Lady Laura, I can promise you that!"

So Johnny did what he was told. And he was told to say his dancing partner for the contest was from out of town, but would be there the night of the contest. He was to put the name Madame Ruby down. He ignored the raised eyebrows and giggles. Being twenty-two, in love, and having a sister like Molly was more, much more than he could handle.

The night of the competition, Molly didn't even ask to go out. She said she was tired and thought she'd go to bed early. Harold, Molly's eleven-year-old brother, had already gone upstairs to bed. The two older brothers, Johnny and Billy, had gone to the music pavilion. Molly's father was working late. Molly's mother raised her eyes from her mending and asked Molly if she were feeling well. Molly said she thought she might be coming down with a cold. Upstairs she put the finishing touches on her costume.

About three quarters of an hour later, Molly decided she'd better check on her mother. Downstairs, her mother was pouring boiling water into the teapot.

"Oh, there ye are, darlin'. Feelin' better? I was just makin' ye a nice hot cup o' tea."

"Oh thanks, Mum. I'll take it up to bed with me. I came down to say goodnight. Are you going to bed?"

"Yes. I'm takin' me tea up, too. I'll leave the key under the mat for yer father and brothers. Do ye want a hot water bottle?"

"No thank you. I'm not a bit cold, just terrible sleepy. Well, goodnight. Thanks for the tea. I'll see you in the mornin'."

"Goodnight, darling. God bless."

Back upstairs in her room, Molly put on the black dress. It was completely unrecognizable. The white lace collar was now red. There was a long red scarf that replaced the soft sash, and there was something very peculiar about the hem. It dipped, long in the back and short in the front—so short in the front you could see Molly's knees! From under the bed Molly brought out a pair of black velvet pumps. They were her mother's; she had 'borrowed' them along with a huge pearl brooch. Earlier, she had attached black satin bows to the shoes. Now she wound the black sash that came with the dress around her head. After securing it, she placed the pearl brooch on the turban just above her forehead. The effect was dramatic, to say the least. Quickly, she took a pot of rouge from the bottom of her dresser and applied it to her cheeks and lips very liberally.

She stepped back from the mirror. She certainly had the figure! There was one more thing: The back of the dress—there wasn't any.

Molly had cut the back of the black dress right out! Her heart gave a jump. Did she have the nerve to go through with this? Never mind that, could she get out of the house! She got her long blue surge coat from the wardrobe and slipped it on. She was ready with one more quick look in the mirror. Just as she was turning from the mirror, her mother walked in.

"What on Earth?"

"Oh Mum, it's all right. I'm feeling so much better. I thought I'd go and watch the dance contest."

"Ye're going out? Oh no, young lady. Ye're not getting out of a sick bed to go watch a dance."

"Oh Mum, I'm not sick. Besides, that's why I've bundled up. You always said to wear a hat and keep your ears warm."

"Even without me glasses, ye look very flushed."

"Oh Mum, please, please? Johnny and Billy are at the pavilion. Just because I'm a girl I have to sit at home? Edith Mona Cafe's mum is letting her go and watch."

"Young lady, I'm not interested what other mothers do. I'm worried about ye. Isn't that my brooch ye have stuck on yer head?"

Just then Harold came running into his sister's bedroom.

"Mummy, Mummy, look what I found on yer bed. It's a letter and it says, M.O.—mother."

Molly tried to grab the letter from Harold and said, "Get out of my room, ye little—here, give me that!"

"No, no, it's not for you. Better hurry. Does Mummy know ye're going dancing?"

"Why, you little bugger. I'll get you for this. GIVE ME THAT LETTER!"

"STOP! Stop this bickering at once. Harold, what on Earth are ye doing out of bed? Ye'll catch your death with nothing on yer feet. Now, what's all this about a letter? Thank ye, Harold."

The mother took the letter from Harold and opened it. As she read it, her face turned quite pale and she sobbed, "Oh dear God, no. This can't be!"

Molly took the letter from her mother's hands and read out loud, "Dear Mother, I know this will be a terrible shock and I'm very sorry. But I am 22 now and must make my own way. Laura and I are going to be married in York. Laura's father is willing to give me a job if I marry Laura in the Church of England. This is what I have decided to do. Good-bye. Yours Truly, Johnny"

Molly's mother collapsed on the bed, Harold was jumping up and down, and Molly was livid.

"He's not marrying her before the contest or I'll kill him!"

With that she stormed out of the bedroom, down the stairs, and out the back door.

At the music pavilion, Johnny was nowhere in sight. Billy, Molly's middle brother, was sitting at a table near the door with his girlfriend, Megan Clayton. Miss Clayton's brother, Joe, was also sitting with them. Around them the contest was getting organized. Contestants were milling around the dance floor and the band members were taking their places.

As the three young people waited for the contest to begin, Joe Clayton was telling his sister and Billy that he had come to a very important decision in his life. He had decided to become a priest. The next day he would be taking the ferry to Ireland to visit a seminary and apply to be admitted for next term. Joe was an extremely good-looking, serious young man. This was not a surprise, but still, his sister and Billy were speechless.

The door to the pavilion flew open and Molly stormed in. She immediately spotted her brother, Billy, and went directly to his table. Without even a hello to any of them, she flung off her coat, grabbed Joe Clayton, pulled him to his feet, and pushed him onto the dance floor.

The music began.

"Ladies and gentlemen, the Beaumaris Music Pavilion is proud to present its first Ballroom Dance Contest. Couple number one, if you please."

Molly pushed Joe in front of the couple who clearly thought they were number one. The house lights were turned down and a spotlight encircled Molly and Joe. Molly placed Joe's right hand squarely on her bare back, and they began to dance.

Meanwhile, Molly's mother came in the door, out of breath, tears rolling down her cheeks, holding Johnny's letter. She too saw her son, Billy, and collapsed in a chair at his table. She was catching her breath and waving the letter at the same time.

At that moment, Molly waltzed by and her mother was confronted with her daughter's naked back as Joe twirled Molly to the music. Her mother sat paralyzed and her face instantly turned the color of cold gray stone, her eyes dilated to small glass saucers, and her mouth became completely unhinged. Slowly, and with great concentration of will, her mother closed her eyes and put a hand over her gapping mouth. But she couldn't keep her eyes closed. She opened her eyes and held her breath as she watched her daughter dip and sway in perfect time in one of the most scandalous dresses the mother had ever seen!

For the briefest of moments Molly's mother fought with all her strength the temptation to acknowledge to herself it was a beautiful costume and her own daughter was dancing sensationally! But then she put both hands over her face and cried to herself, "Oh God, forgive Molly. This is all my fault. I am too lenient with her and now my son has run away! Oh God, I've failed you miserably!"

Meanwhile all eyes were popping out as those two young people danced. So perfect was the music, the dress, and the dancers. They were waltzing exquisitely. Then the music changed and they did the two-step, then the fox trot and the Charleston. By this time, everyone was clapping and cheering. Suddenly the house lights were turned on, signaling time was up, but the whole audience was shouting, "MORE, MORE!"

The announcer said they must continue with the contest. The music started again and the next couple began to dance. But the spell was broken. Molly's mother sucked in air audibly. Billy was fanning his mother and trying to get her to drink some lemon squash.

"Mum, Mum, please take a sip; are ye all right?"

Little Harold had come in and was standing by his mother completely unnoticed. Suddenly he piped up, "Johnny ran away with a hussy, and Molly's going to kill him. And Mummy's going to kill them both!"

With that, his mother started crying again and held up the letter. Billy took the letter and read it as his mother sobbed, "Yer brother has run away with a Pro...Pro...Pro...Protestant! And your sister dances half-naked with a priest! What did I do to deserve this? Holy Mother of God, forgive them! Please, please take me home, Billy. I'm not speaking to yer brother or yer sister, the slut!"

Megan Clayton put her arm around Mrs. Lewis and said, "Joe isn't a priest yet, Mrs. Lewis. He's just thinking of becoming one."

"Aye, and he has a lot more to think about now, doesn't he? How will I ever face yer mother?"

Billy put the letter down and said, "Does Dad know?"

"I don't know. The letter was only addressed to me."

"Right. Well, Mum, ye know Johnny's not been happy for a long time. He's always wanted to get out of Beaumaris."

"Aye, I know. It's just I can't bear to let him go."

Suddenly Will, Molly's and the boys' father, stood at the table. He had come straight from work. He looked very out of place in his overalls and boots, but he pulled a chair over from another table and sat anyway. He looked at his wife and said, "Are ye all right? Now, I don't want ye upsetting yerself. The boy come to me and I told 'em. Go, go if ye must. Ye know as well as I, we won't stand in any of 'em's way. Come on, then, I'll take ye home. This music—it's, well, it's so bloody loud I can't hear meself think."

The two of them stood up and moved towards the door. Little Harold ran after his mother, pulling on her arm and shouting, "Mummy, Mummy, look. Molly and Joe won the contest. Look, they're giving Molly that silver cup!"

His mother pulled her arm away and continued towards the door.

"I'm not interested. She's not my daughter. I disown her!"

Suddenly Harold dropped his arm and turned toward the platform and said very loudly, "Mummy, Mummy, look. Molly's crying—they're taking the silver cup *back*!"

His mother whirled around and shouted, "Oh dear God! What's going on? What are they doing to my child? Let me through, let me through. I'm her mother. What's the trouble? I demand to know!"

"Oh, Mrs. Lewis, we've just been notified your daughter is underage. I'm awfully sorry, but we cannot allow Mr. Clayton and your daughter to win the contest."

"She was the best, wasn't she? Very poorly run! Very poorly run. Come Molly, I'll take ye home. There, there, darling, don't cry. Here, use me handkerchief. Ye and Joe were clearly the winners. Why didn't ye tell me ye could dance like that? I had no idea. And for God's sake, put yer coat on before yer dad sees the back of that dress and ye catch yer death of cold."

 **1937**

MOLLY AND BILL

"Face it Molly, you're an old maid!"

Molly was furious.

"You're 29 years old and haven't a prayer in hell of catching a husband in this town. 'Your way or no way' precedes you. Face facts, little sister, you need to marry a man ten thousand miles away!"

Molly saw red! The most immediate thing she could lay her hands on was the back door. She opened it and slammed it with both hands.

"Damn, damn, damn!" she said under her breath.

Immediately she composed herself, in case Mary Anne, her mother, came running down the stairs. Her mother didn't, so Molly picked up her purse and left, this time leaving the back door wide open.

All the way down Stanley Street Molly fumed.

"I'll show him! Old maid, indeed! Come hell or high water, I'll be married and out of this godforsaken place by the time I'm thirty. And that's a vow, big brother. I'll bloody well show you!"

She turned the corner onto Church Street and made her way down past the medieval church of St. Mary and St. Nicholas, to Castle Street and the Victorian built hotel, arriving a few minutes after the hour.

Molly Lewis was the new bookkeeper and front desk clerk at the Bulkeley Arms Hotel, in the little seaside town of Beaumaris, on the Isle of Anglesey, in North Wales.

A few minutes after the same hour on the same day, Bill Lewis, an older but very dapper Welsh-American gentleman, was maneuvering his immaculate American Ford sedan across the Menai Suspension Bridge onto the Isle of Anglesey, North Wales. The car was headed straight for the picturesque town of Beaumaris and the Bulkeley Arms Hotel.

Bill had come back to the old country for a well-deserved holiday. Thirty-five years prior, he had left the family farm in mid-Wales and immigrated to Canada. Not for him, Canada, too cold, and the only work had been on farms—as bad or worse than Wales.

He had walked off his first job in Saskatchewan and somehow gotten himself to Vancouver, British Columbia. Finding work in the port city had not been hard. He was young, easy to get along with, and quite clever at playing cards. But it was not long before he found himself shanghaied on a ship to Singapore.

After a day at sea, a ferocious storm turned the ship back and Bill found himself in the United States of America. While in Seattle, Bill jumped ship and never looked back. Not wanting to be shanghaied again, he kept moving. All down the coast of Washington, Oregon and most of California, Bill played cards in the back room of saloons. He kept a low profile, never taking unnecessary risks or staying too long in one place. That is, until he came to a town called Salinas, California, a hundred miles south of San Francisco. Bill loved Salinas. Not too hot, not too cold and just far enough from the sea.

The liquor lord of Salinas hired Bill to deal in the back rooms in several of his saloons. Finally coming out of Prohibition and the Great Depression, business was good, very good. Men needed escape.

While John Steinbeck wrote about the people in the Salinas Valley, Bill played cards with the men, listened to their troubles, took their money and, on occasion, personally lent money to them.

In 1937, several loans were repaid and Bill was flush. He bought a new car and drove to New York. On a whim, he decided to take himself and his new car back to the old country for a quick visit.

There was a problem when it was discovered Bill was not in the country legally. Luckily for Bill (or, in light of later events, perhaps not) he had joined the newly formed AAA automobile club just before his road trip east. The automobile club took it upon itself to wire the Salinas National Bank. A telegram was immediately returned to say Mr. Lewis was a trusted customer and he had $2000 deposited in the Salinas Bank. Passport, visa, and passage on the next available ship sailing for England were waiting for Bill the next morning.

They met at the reception desk of the Bulkeley Arms Hotel. Before Bill had time to get out of his car (the likes of which few had seen in Beaumaris) and up the hotel steps, word had spread he was an American millionaire. Molly couldn't have been more charming. She saw to it that he had the room Queen Victoria had slept in a hundred years ago, and she arranged for tea to be brought to him in the lounge. They laughed over having the same last name. But they both agreed—good Welsh stock. Bill asked her to have tea with him and she accepted.

Bill was enchanted. A sweet Welsh girl half his age, living with her parents and working hard at her job. Certainly nothing like the American women he had met and heard about from the men in the back room of the saloons. From what he gathered, American women had completely forgotten their place, nagging their husbands to buy houses, washing machines, vacuum cleaners; any newfangled gadget to get out of a little hard work. Although he was too much the gentleman to say it, he truly thought American women should never have been given the vote.

He was definitely not interested in an American woman of any age. But a young Welsh girl, who knew her place, who was not afraid of hard work, who could cook, clean and take care of him, who knew nothing of newfangled gadgets or fancy clothes—Bill realized this was the kind of wife he had been looking for all his life.

Bill felt very sorry for the ex-king of England. The king had lost his kingdom because he had been completely outsmarted and hoodwinked by the fast, free thinking, American woman, Wallace Simpson. This would never happen to Bill Lewis!

By the end of the first week, Bill was eating dinner with Molly and her parents. Molly stopped and bought a very special Welsh bread called Bara Brith from the bakery. Bill hadn't had Bara Brith since he'd left the farm in Wales thirty-five years before. He assumed Molly had made it especially for him. No one said otherwise.

The Lodge, the house where Molly's parents lived and Molly and her brothers had grown-up, was completely made of stone. Molly's father and mother kept a coal fire (the only source of heat) constantly in the kitchen. Molly assured Bill she was more at home in the kitchen than any other room in the house.

On the other hand, Bill told Molly and her family he was a retired businessman. No one thought to ask what business.

For the next week, Bill had visions of home-cooked meals, starched, ironed white shirts, and a house so clean he could eat off the kitchen floor. Molly had visions of a huge mansion with a cook and housemaids galore.

Just after Bill left the hotel to go back to California, Molly burst into the house shouting, "Mum, Mum, he's asked me to marry him and I said, yes!"

"Oh, Molly, no! Ye've only known him barely two weeks! My God, Father, he's as old as yer father and me!"

"Mum, I don't jolly well care how old he is. He's going to send me a ticket to America. I'll be married when I get there."

"Oh, Molly, I can't let ye do this. Marriage is permanent; there's no turning back. What if it's not anything like ye think? What will ye do? Ye'll have no family to turn to—ye'll be all alone. I don't think ye realize how hard life can be for a woman."

"Mum, wild horses can't stop me. Nothing you say or do will change my mind. **I am** going to America!"

"Oh Molly, what if there's a war? It won't be safe on the water."

"Mum, you're not listening to me. Bugger the war, bugger the Germans! I don't bloody well care; if Wallace Simpson can come over here and nab a British King, I can certainly go over there and marry an old Welsh millionaire! Besides, you'll pray for me. I'll be fine."

"Good God, give me strength!"

The ticket to America came. On September 7, 1937, Molly boarded the ship bound for New York. Her mother saw her off and, as she said good-bye, she slipped an open return ticket into Molly's pocket. "Yer dad says we won't stand in anyone's way, so go, be safe—and use this in case anything goes wrong! God bless."

Barely a week later, Molly arrived in New York. She took the train to Reno, Nevada. On September 15th, Molly married Bill in Reno's Catholic Cathedral. Bill took Molly to live in Salinas, California.

Arriving in Salinas, Molly was at first fascinated with everyone owning a car, heated rooms, electric lights, telephones and indoor bathrooms. But it soon dawned on her that Bill was not a millionaire, nowhere near one, and he had no intention of ever buying her a house.

It dawned on Bill that Molly was not the sweet, innocent girl he thought he married. She was totally erratic in the kitchen and it all depended on her mood if he got a meal. He quickly learned how to get a clean shirt: he had to go to the laundry, pay, and pick up all their clean and ironed laundry. Molly repeatedly told him she had absolutely no interest in a newfangled washing machine or an electric iron.

When Molly became pregnant, an old lady who lived in the duplex next door gave Molly a blow-by-blow description of what was to come. That did it. Molly was on the next available ship home to her mother. Just before she left, Molly said to her husband, "I'll be back. See that you buy a house while I'm gone and see that it's bigger than this dump. And keep it tidy; I don't want to come back to a tip!"

Some weeks later, Bill tripped over the newfangled vacuum cleaner as he got up from writing the rent check. Saying a word he ordinarily never used, he walked into the kitchen piled high with dirty dishes. He poured himself two-day-old coffee into an already used mug and sat at the kitchen table. How had he let this happen? How had she learned to out-bluff him at every turn?

The doorbell rang. It was Western Union: "Bill and Molly Lewis are the parents of their first child, a daughter, Marion."

 **1938**

MARION

"Molly, she's beautiful. What are you going to call her?"

"Beautiful? She looks like a drowned rat! She has no eyelashes, fingernails or toenails."

"Oh, Molly, the doctor says they'll grow. It's because she was so early. What about her name?"

"Oh, bloody hell, I don't know. She was supposed to be William David. I can't think, she's worn me out. Would you take her downstairs so I can rest. Why is she crying?"

"Molly, she's a baby. Babies are supposed to cry. I'll take her downstairs and give her a bottle by the fire. The doctor left a special formula for her; he wants me to feed her every hour. He'll be back tomorrow to check on you and the baby. Now, you've strict orders to stay in bed and rest.

"But quick, darling, here's a piece of paper and pencil. Write out what you want to say to your husband. I'll see it gets to Western Union. He'll be anxious to hear the baby is here and is all right."

"I really don't feel like it. Oh, all right. I better get it over with. He has to know it's not William David!"

Mary Anne carries her brand new granddaughter and the message for the telegram downstairs. Laying the message on the kitchen table and holding the baby in one hand, she heats a bottle on the gas stove with her other, talking to the baby the whole while.

"Now, how am I going to get a telegram to your father in America? Right, I'll ask Father Brady if he'll drop it off. The doctor said he'll tell Father of your birth and ask him to drop by. I want ye to be baptized as quick as possible. God knows you're a wee thing and your mother's had a bit of a hard time. I'll have to feed you for the time being."

Mary Anne takes the bottle from the pan of water, turns off the gas, then awkwardly shakes the milk on her wrist to test if it's too hot. Satisfied it's not, she sits in the wooden rocking chair by the fire and gives the bottle to the baby.

Mary Anne bends over, kisses the baby, and whispers in the baby's ear.

"Can I believe I'm holding my own daughter's daughter? Oh dear God, when I was young and in Ireland, they took my wee baby boy from me. With my every breath, I felt so much pain, so much utter hopelessness!

"I came to Wales a broken woman. God and your Grandfather gave me my life back.

"But as the years went by I became petrified on the one hand and determined on the other that my own daughter, Molly, would never suffer the way I did because I was a weak woman and had no rights. And now I'm worried and determined for you, too.

"You know, I've a mind to call ye 'Marion.' Molly won't mind. That's another name for Mary. I'll pray night and day for you and your mother to go back safely across the ocean, to a safer land than this. Before your mother wakes, I'll give you a blessing, wee one. May it bring you to safe harbors throughout your life!"

QUEEN MARY 2

The QM2 is so modern and huge; it is like, and yet, nothing like, any of the ships I remember being on as a child.

Yesterday was our first full day at sea. I stood on one of the forward decks and let the wind have at me. It blew my hair to bits and, as I held on to the rail, I could feel the ocean spray hit my face. Suddenly I had an incredible sense of déjà vu with the ship, the wind, the sea. I felt all three asking me, *What has taken you so long?*

I am my mother's daughter. I love being on the ocean, well, the Atlantic Ocean. This will be my sixth time crossing on an ocean liner. My very first time as an adult, and with my husband, I couldn't be more thrilled!

As a child, being on the water, I remember feeling the power and the strength of the sea. It frightened me, still does. Yet if I stood, stand on deck, with the wind in my face, gazing out at the sea's immensity, mesmerized by its perpetual motion, it would always give me a sense of overwhelming wonder and peace, still does.

It boggles my mind that no matter how much time evaporates from my life, the ocean has been, is, and will be, long after I disappear from this earth.

When I was little, on a ship and scared, I'd imagine I was floating on the face of God; I'd look down at the water and ask God to push us with his nose and give the ship strength to get us safely across to the other side.

When we lived with Grandma and Grandpa, I always remember Grandma asking God or His mother for strength. Mom would be yelling at Grandma and I knew Grandma was just as mad at Mom, but Grandma never yelled back and she never yelled at us children. All Grandma would do when she was upset was look up and say, "Dear Mother of God, give me strength."

SECOND DAY ON QUEEN MARY 2

Today, the wind has fallen off and the vast ocean gently bobs up and down. From the horizon, gray billowing clouds, are spreading a huge safe canopy that the Queen, me and my scary new computer, are sailing straight under.

I've found the most amazing place to think, remember, and write starting at seven thirty in the morning. It's the Commodore Bar, directly beneath the bridge. I've ordered a cup of tea and I'm sitting in a very comfortable chair, with a front row view of the great bow of the

QM2, slicing confidently, methodically, through boundless water.

I wish I felt that confident in my progress. I finished the stories that happened before I was born, based on what I was told or overheard from my mother, grandmother, grandfather and other relatives.

Ironically, I'm more worried about writing my own memories. They are all so intertwined with my mother's multiple, conflicting accounts of many of the same events.

Can I be strong enough to tell *my* truth, not hers?

Marion Lewis Besmehn

PART II

GROWING UP WITH MOLLY

Crossing The Ocean

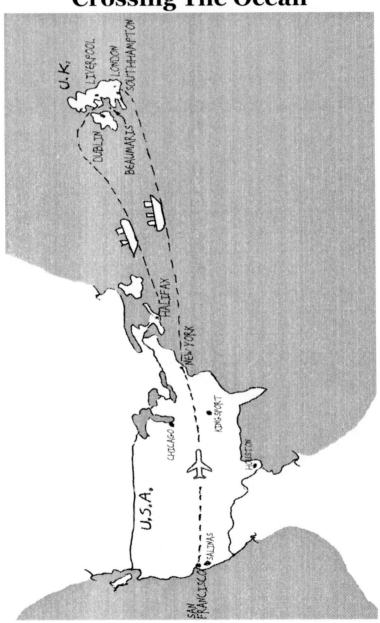

 **1943**

HOBNAILS AND RING

In 1943, my mother, brother and I were living at the Lodge in Beaumaris, on the Isle of Angelesey, North Wales. The Lodge was my grandparents' home.

The Lodge was a small stone house at the beginning of Stanley Street. In the old days, the Lodge was a sort of guard house with a huge, closed iron gate that the lodge keeper would open to invited guests to the manor house at the top of the hill.

In 1943, the Williams-Bulkeley family, who had owned much of Beaumaris since the middle ages, were no longer living in the manor house; it had been turned over to Polish soldiers. The huge iron gate outside the Lodge had been taken down for the war effort. But my grandfather was still in charge of the grounds and the forest surrounding the manor house. After the First World War, Grandpa and his family had been given the Lodge to live in.

I remember my grandma (Mary Anne) and grandpa (Will) and my mother (Molly) telling me that I had a father across the ocean in America. They said that I had already been to America once and that someday my Mommy, Billy and I were going to go there again, to live. I had no idea what or where they were talking about.

The only father I knew was my grandfather, and I adored him. Every night, Grandpa walked in the door, hung his cap and coat on the peg, then walked across the kitchen floor to his big wooden chair by the fireplace. It was then that my brother, Billy, and I would beg Grandpa to let us help him take off his huge boots. Grandpa's boots were very special. They had nails on the bottom of the soles for traction. We could always hear Grandpa coming up the gravel path in his hobnail boots. It was that loud, gravely, crunching sound that Billy and I listened for every evening.

Billy was only three years old, so he was still a baby, but he loved Grandpa as much as I did. Every night my brother would not go to sleep until Grandpa went up the stairs and said, "goodnight" and left his hobnail boots by the side of his crib. When Grandpa came down the stairs from saying goodnight to Billy, that was my special time with Grandpa. He would scoop me up in his arms, sit me on his knee in his big wooden chair by the fireplace and recite Mother Goose to me.

Humpty Dumpty sat on a wall;
Humpty Dumpty had a great fall....

Grandpa would open his legs and drop me through, holding me tight all the way to the floor, then pull me up quickly to start all over again. I especially loved *Sing a Song of Sixpence*. When Grandpa came to the end of the poem, he would raise his hand high above his head and sweep it down as he said,

> *The maid was in the garden*
> *Hanging up the clothes—*
> *When along came a blackbird*
> *And pecked off her nose.*

He would gently tug at my nose and say, "See, I have ye nose now!"

He'd put his thumb between his middle finger and his index finger and hold it up for me to see.

"Put it back, Grandpa! Put it back," I'd cry. He would always make a great gesture of putting my nose back in place.

One evening I was sitting on his knee, squealing in delight as he recited my favorite nursery rhymes, when there was a loud knock on the back door. My grandmother was standing next to the fire and had the poker in her hand. My mother was just coming into the kitchen and exclaimed, "Who on earth can that be this time of night?"

Grandma held the red hot poker over the fire and said, "Aye, I don't like it. It's bad news—I can feel it in me bones!"

My mother opened the door and old Mr. Williams from down the road stepped in.

"Good evenin' to ye...." He looked to my grandmother first and nodded, "Mrs. Lewis."

Then he looked at my mother, "Mrs. Lewis."

He was holding his cap in his hand and looking very uncomfortable. My grandmother, wiping her hands on her apron, walked towards him saying, "Come in, Mr. Williams, come in. Will ye have a cuppa tea?"

"No, no, Mrs. Lewis, thank ye. I can't stay." Then he looked directly at my grandfather.

"I'm afraid I've come for ye, Will."

I could feel my grandfather's hands tighten around my waist.

"What's the trouble, John?"

"Aye, we've just got word on the wireless—the Gerries are on their way to bomb Menai Bridge. We've got to get whoever's left in the village to stand guard the night."

My grandmother threw up her hands and said, "Good God in heaven, ye can't be thinkin' of leaving us, Dad, we'll be needing ye here!"

My grandfather gently lifted me to the floor and then stood up. He didn't look at any of us, but he spoke to Mr. Williams as he crossed the kitchen.

"Right. Give me a minute to get me boots and gun."

As soon as my grandfather left the room, my grandmother spoke up.

"This is ridiculous, Mr. Williams. What are a bunch of old men goin' to do against German aeroplanes? And what if they bomb the village instead of the bridge?"

"I'm sorry, Mrs. Lewis, I've got to go. These are the Home Guards orders and we've all got to do our best. Tell Mr. Lewis to meet in front of the church as quick as he can. Goodnight to ye." He put his cap on his head and let himself out the door.

I was still standing next to Grandpa's chair. I climbed back up in his chair and sat very still. After a few minutes my grandfather came back in the kitchen. He had on his hobnail boots and his Home Guard uniform. He was carrying a gun with a long knife at the end of the barrel in one hand, and in the other, he had a funny-looking, old, dented, tin helmet. He leaned the gun against the wall and put the helmet on. Fastening the strap under his chin, he spoke to my grandmother and my mother.

"I want ye to check all the blackouts on the windows. Now, if ye hear any bombing at all, I want ye to get into the coal cellar. Do ye understand?"

Grandma nodded her head and said under her breath, "You're to meet in front of the church."

"Right, I'm off."

He picked up his gun, opened the door and was gone. I could hear the noise of the hobnail boots crunching on the gravel getting fainter and fainter. I cried, "Grandpa, Grandpa! Come back—come back you didn't...."

But it was too late. He didn't hear me; no one heard me. Suddenly my mother spoke.

"All right, I'm going upstairs to check the windows." Looking straight at me my mother said sharply, "You, get up the stairs to bed."

Grandma said, "I'll put the kettle on, let the child stay while we have our tea, I want her with us for a little while."

My mother was not happy. I knew she wanted me upstairs and out of the way. She picked up a candle, lit it, and walked out of the kitchen. I turned myself around and put my hands tight around the back rungs while I stuck both feet completely through. I was holding on for dear life. My grandmother came over to me and said, "Aye, child, it's a bad night. Perhaps you and I can say a prayer your grandfather will be safe? Both of us have to ask God to make us strong so we can do His will."

I reached through the chair rung and tugged on her pinny, "Grandma, grandma, when's grandpa coming back?

She looked down at me and I could see tears in her eyes as she said, "Aye, child, I don't know.

With this, I grabbed hold of the chair rungs and screamed, "I want my Grandpa!" The chair fell over backward. At the moment I yelled and the chair fell, the gaslight over the kitchen table flickered and almost went out. The fall silenced me; I had not hurt myself, as my feet hit the floor first, but I had scared myself half to death. I watched my grandmother as she made the sign of the cross and wiped the tears from her face. In the dim, eerie light, in one fell swoop, she picked up the chair with me on it. She said, "Aye, child, it's all right, it's all right."

My mother ran into the room.

"What in God's name is going on in here? Now look what you've done—the baby's awake. Get out of that chair and up to bed before I give you something to really cry about."

Grandma spoke, "No, Molly. Leave the child be. She's upset as I am. She's going to stay with me and we'll both pray for your father's safe return."

My mother looked at me and then at her mother and said, "Don't be ridiculous, She's going straight up those stairs to bed. I want peace while I have my tea."

"Molly the child's upset. Her Grandfather left without saying 'good-bye' and she and I are going to ask God for strength for whatever happens. This is bad business. I believe God listens to a child's prayer and she's a smart girl and knows the danger your father's in. Haven't I been through the First World War? Prayer is the only thing we women can do. Why don't you take your tea up to bed to be with the baby?"

"No, she can go upstairs and look in on the baby."

"I'm yer mother. And I'll thank ye to do as ye're told in me house."

My mother didn't wait for her tea. She stomped out of the kitchen. I could hear her feet going up the stairs and the soft whimpering of the baby. Grandma gave me a weak cup of tea with a little sugar and milk. She poured the hot tea into the saucer so I wouldn't burn my mouth. While Grandma and I drank our tea, she told me the story of losing her wedding ring down the drain when Grandpa was away fighting in the first World War.

I loved the gold band Grandma always wore. I turned it on her finger as she told me that the ring I was turning was not the one she lost. When she lost the first one it was gone forever. She said she was sure it was a sign from God that Grandpa had been killed. "Aye child, ye never know what God is going to do. You have to always, always, ask God for strength to bear what he has in mind. When your Grandpa turned up at me door, you could have knocked me over with a feather! God answered me prayers! Then didn't I have to send to Birmingham for another gold band? Took me two years to save enough money. This be the one. Perhaps someday you'll have it. I hope you remember to always ask God for strength to do his will."

Before Grandma turned the gaslight off and lit a candle on the kitchen table, she got two thick blankets and a pillow out of the cupboard.

She asked me if I wanted to stay with her or did I want to go upstairs? "Oh Grandma, please let me stay with you." Grandma put a pillow behind me on Grandpa's chair and a blanket over me. I snuggled down and watched Grandma take a set of large black rosary beads out of her apron pocket. She made the sign of the cross over me, then she sat at the kitchen table and started whispering Hail Mary's—both hands clutching the black beads as they clicked between her fingers.

The next thing I remember is opening my eyes to pitch black and hearing a loud, droning sound overhead. Grandma's voice came through the blackness. It scared me; I couldn't think where I was.

"Aye, that'll be them."

"Grandma? Grandma, where are you? What's that noise!" Grandma was beside me. I felt better and I knew where I was. "What's that noise? It sounds like bumble bees!"

"No child, it's German aeroplanes come to bomb the bridge your Grandfather's guarding."

I remember crying, "Grandpa! Grandpa! I want my Grandpa!"

"Aye child, I know, I know. We must pray to be strong."

The noise of the airplanes began to die out. Grandma went over to the window and pulled the blackout off. I could see the outline of the panes of glass, but it was still black outside. Suddenly we saw a small burst of light in the distance, and another and another. I could hear a faint popping sound. Grandmother said the Our Father and I joined her the best I could remember:

> *...and forgive us our trespasses, as we forgive those who trespass against us; and lead us not into temptation, but deliver us from evil.*

Then it was over. The lights and the popping sound stopped. I must have started shivering because my grandmother came over to me and put the blanket that was around her shoulders over me. She knelt down and put her arms around me.

"It's a bad night for all of us, child." Grandma stood up and again got her black rosary out of her pocket and started pacing up and down saying the Hail Mary's in a loud, strong voice, back and forth, back and forth, as the beads clicked and clacked in front of my chair.

The next thing I remember was opening my eyes to the kitchen flooded with light and hearing that wonderful, gravely crunching sound

Grandpa's boots always made! "Grandpa! Grandpa!" I shouted.

Grandma was at the kitchen table with her eyes closed, head on the table, still clutching the rosary beads. Again the crackling crunching noise!

I shouted at the top of my voice, "Grandpa's home! Grandpa's home!"

Grandma's head came straight up off the table and without hesitation she said, "Jesus, Mary, and Joseph!

The doorknob turned and Grandpa walked in!

Grandpa, putting his gun down and unfastening the strap of his tin helmet, looked at her and said, "Mother, where's me tea?"

My mother came into the kitchen with my baby brother in her arms. Billy saw Grandpa, put his arms up and said, "*Pa, Pa!*"

Grandpa took Billy from my mother's arms and said, "We watched as the Jerries come out of the sky and dropped their bloody bombs, but don't ye know? Everyone one of 'em missed the bridge by a quarter of a mile! The whole ruddy payload in the drink and not one of 'em hurt a fly! Old Reverend Dan, the retired Methodist minister, he was out there with us all night; he said it be a miracle and we should all get down on our knees and thank God for whoever spent the night praying for our side!"

By this time I was standing on Grandpa's chair jumping up and down.

"Grandpa, Grandpa, ye come home, ye come home!"

He came toward me and with one arm holding Billy, he put the other arm around me and said, "Aye, I come home. Where ye think I'd be goin' this time of day—*dancing*?"

"Grandpa, ye left last night and ye took me nose with ye. I can't get off yer chair without me nose. Please Grandpa, put it back, put it back!"

And he did. He always did! And I saw out of the corner of my eye, Grandma turning her gold wedding ring around her finger, looking up at the ceiling and whispering, "Thank God."

1943

LIFE JACKETS

October 1943 was the first time I remember going to America with my mother and my brother, Billy. World War II was raging. I had just turned five years old; Billy was three.

When we boarded the ship in Liverpool, we were told there would be a hundred war ships accompanying us across the North Atlantic. Everyone on the ship was ordered to stay dressed and ready to evacuate the ship at a moment's notice in case the enemy hit us with a torpedo under the water, or we were hit from the air by an enemy plane. There were no soldiers on board our ship. When I looked through our ship's railing, I could see lots and lots of ships surrounding us with big guns, pointing up to the sky.

On our ship there were stewards dressed in white jackets. They came and cleaned our cabin every day, and they served the food in the dining room. Mommy loved the service and the food. She said she had never seen so much food since before the war. She loved going to dinner every evening.

There were only twelve of us passengers on board, and four were children. Every evening we took turns sitting with two or three different people at a round table with a white linen tablecloth, silver knives and forks and beautiful china. Billy and I were never allowed to touch anything on the table. We were not allowed to sit with the other two children. Mommy said that children are to be seen but never heard. She gave us strict orders; we were to sit quietly and eat fancy food on the plain dishes with spoons she asked the steward to bring from the kitchen. She said she could not trust us not to break something; she would *die* of embarrassment. Billy and I hated the fancy food. All we wanted was the food Grandma had given us: plain bread and honey, a soft boiled egg, mashed potatoes and carrots from Grandpa's victory garden.

Mommy was very upset with us and said we were very ungrateful, spoiled children and she was ashamed of us. My first memories of being seasick took place on this ship, in the middle of the ocean, but it only happened when Mommy was furious with Billy and me.

On the first night, Mommy enthralled everyone at the dinner table with her stories of how her husband in America, a retired businessman, had moved the powers that be to get us on this ship as he was so sure he would die before he ever saw his son, Billy. Mommy said he'd seen me. She said I went to America with her, when I was five months old. I had no memory of this and had no idea who the man was.

The next night at dinner, with different people, she told how she had written to Megan Lloyd George, the daughter of the ex-prime minister, David Lloyd George. David Lloyd George was Welsh just like we were.

The ex-prime minister had retired, and his daughter was now a member of parliament. Mommy said they were our neighbors, with their family home practically next door to us on the Isle of Anglesey. So she said she had written to Megan in London and had explained how she had been caught completely off guard by the war while she was visiting her mother and father in Wales. Because of the war she couldn't get back to her husband in time for their son to be born. At the table Mommy said, "I wrote Megan, and told her that my son is three years old and his father is quite a bit older than me. He has never laid eyes on his only son! Is there any way on Earth you can get us to America before my husband dies without seeing the son he waited for all his life?" Mommy said her good friend and neighbor, Megan Lloyd George, personally got us on this ship.

I had never heard these stories told this way before, so I was all ears. Billy always fell asleep at the dinner table.

When we got back in our cabin after dinner of the third night, Mommy told Billy and me, "Oh, bugger the Germans, I'm taking a bath and I'm not sleeping in my clothes!" While Mommy was in the bathtub, the siren went off. It really scared Billy and me, but Mommy was furious. When we finally got up to the deck where all the passengers were assembled, I noticed everyone was wearing a life jacket. Then I heard the loudspeaker they were all listening to. It said, "Ladies and gentlemen, this is just a drill." I knew from the look on Mommy's face she was furious. She tightened her grip on our hands, turned us around and marched us back down to our cabin.

When an officer stopped Mommy to ask why we didn't have our lifejackets on, Mommy hit the roof (that's what Grandma always said when Mommy starts yelling really loud). "When your bloody stupid siren went off, my two children were fast asleep, and I was just having a quick wash! There were no lifejackets in sight! Tell me, young man, do you and the Captain stay up at night planning the worst possible time for your bloody drills for a mother traveling alone with two babies?"

The officer said he was very sorry and said he would have three lifejackets sent immediately to our cabin. Mommy hardly had time to stick the ones that were in our cabin under the bed before a steward named Jack appeared. He came in and showed us how to put on the lifejackets. When Jack found our lifejackets under the bed, Mommy said we children must have been playing with them; she told Jack that when the siren went off, it upset her so much she didn't think to look under the bed. I knew from her eyes I was to keep my mouth shut. Billy was asleep on the bed.

Next morning after breakfast, Jack showed us which lifeboat was ours, and he even took the tarpaulin off and lifted Billy and me into the lifeboat. The next time the siren blasted, Jack came to help us with our lifejackets and take us where we needed to go. The siren blasted a lot and Jack always came to help us. He said we were really lucky that they were all only drills. Billy and I loved Jack.

Our ship, and all the other ships with us, zigzagged across the North Atlantic Ocean for twenty-one days, from Liverpool to Halifax, Nova Scotia.

One of the passengers, a Mr. Patterson, walked Billy and me around and around the deck every day while Mommy had a steward bring a blanket to wrap around her as she sat in a deck chair, reading a book. Billy and I tried waving to the other ships with the big guns, but nobody waved back.

Mommy was the star of our ship. Everyone knew her and loved listening to her stories. I did too. I had never seen or heard Mommy tell most of these stories before.

Without Grandma and Grandpa, Mommy was completely different. Other than our walks with Mr. Patterson, Billy and I were in our cabin to take endless rests. We were forbidden to complain or make noise. Mommy drilled me on how I was to answer anyone who spoke to me. I was never to initiate a conversation with an adult. If Mr. Patterson said, "Hello Marion, how are you?" I was always, always to answer, "Good-day, Mr. Patterson, I am very well, thank you. How are you, today?" If I did not say those exact words, then I would be in trouble. I was to watch Billy and answer for him if he was spoken to. Mommy said all her rules did not apply to Billy, as he was still a baby and a boy.

We landed safely in Halifax and took a train to Salinas, California.

1944

SALINAS, CALIFORNIA

When our train arrived in Salinas, California, a man met us at the train station. Mommy said it was our Daddy. But Mommy's not too happy. She wants Daddy to buy a house. He said that houses cost too much money and next year they'll be cheaper. Mommy made the man rent a house on Lorimer Street.

I was so scared the first day of kindergarten that I started to cry on the way to the school. Mommy got really mad and started shaking me to stop crying. An older girl came up behind us. Mommy asked her if she knew where I was to go. She said her name was Joan Breen and she said she knew where the kindergarten class was. Mommy and Billy went home and I went with Joan Breen.

Everything was okay after that. I met my new teacher, Miss Smith. She was really nice to me and I stopped crying. I really, really liked kindergarten even though Mommy said it was just playing and not really school.

As soon as I was old enough Mommy put me in first grade at Sacred Heart School. It's further away than kindergarten but I know how to walk to it. I got in a lot of trouble my first day walking home, though. It was sprinkling, so I had on my boots and raincoat, but as I was leaving the classroom I noticed I'd forgot to put on my new sweater under my raincoat, so I just grabbed it and carried it home with me. Mommy and Billy came to meet me and when Mommy saw I was carrying my sweater she got really, really mad and started yelling at me from across the street.

I tried to explain that Sister had been reading a story about two little children who got lost in the woods. When the bell rang we begged Sister to hurry and finish the story. We all wanted to know if the children found their way home. Sister kept reading; I think she wanted to know what happened as much as we did. It had a happy ending. The children's dog, "Duke," found them and showed them the way home.

We all loved the story but Sister said we were really late, so please put our coats and boots on as quick as possible. Sister was clicking her clicker as fast and as loud as she could and the boys were having a lot of trouble with their boots and coats. We girls wanted to show Sister how fast we could be putting on our boots and raincoats and sitting quietly at our desks waiting to be dismissed. That's why I forgot my sweater.

Mommy says she's not interested in excuses. She says I'm stupid and thoughtless. Lots of times Mommy tears up my homework because she says I do it wrong. I try to tell her that was the way my teacher said to do it. Mommy says that is not the right way.

Billy and I love Salinas but Mommy doesn't. Billy is too young to go to school but he has friends in the neighborhood that he plays with all day long. I love school. I have a friend, Joan Martella, in my class I walk home with her everyday.

Mommy's yelling more and more at Billy, me and Daddy. She says we are going back to Beaumaris; she's sick of Salinas. She got a job so she can buy the tickets. She works at a hotel. After school I am to stay in the house and look after Billy until she comes home. We are not to tell anybody she is working.

One day, it seemed she was never coming home. Billy was crying, so I told him to put his coat on and we would walk up Central Avenue to meet her coming home. Mommy never came down the street and while we were waiting for her a policeman stopped and told us he'd take us home. Mommy was home when we got there. She told the policeman she was just next door and I had misunderstood. She gave me her 'look' and I knew I was not to say a word. It reminded me of when we were on the boat and the lifejackets.

When we got in the house Mommy said she couldn't trust me to do one thing right. Everything I do is wrong she says. In fact, she says, if I ever do anything right she'll fly a flag from our house. I looked at Billy when she said that, thinking he would find it funny, but lately as soon as Mommy starts yelling he falls asleep. I wish I could do that.

Mommy is very unhappy. The man still won't buy Mommy a house. Mommy is yelling at him and us all the time. He doesn't yell at her; he just walks out the door of the house that Mommy made the man rent for us. He comes home, usually before we wake up in the morning, but he never talks to Billy and me.

Mommy says the three worst regrets in her life are: marrying the man she says is our father, having us children and never being able to sail on the Queen Mary. Every day she thinks about these three things, and she starts yelling all over again.

When we are around other people, Mommy makes everyone laugh. She always has a story to tell. But, she never tells us the funny stories.

I am so aware of anything and everything my mother says. I don't understand how she can be one way with other people and so different when she's alone with Billy and me. She tells me she is mad at God for getting her into this mess with us kids and with the man who says he's Daddy. Well, I've never actually heard him say he's Daddy, but Mommy says he is and she makes us call him that.

Even though she says she is mad at God, we always go to Mass every Sunday. Grandma is from Ireland and a Catholic. So are Mommy, Billy and me. Mommy's God and the God I am learning about from my first grade teacher, Sister Robert Julie, seem to me very different.

Sister Robert Julie says that there is a God up in Heaven who loves everyone on Earth very much; if we try to love back and do what is right and never try to hurt anyone, everything will be okay, even when we die. Sister says people who do really bad things, like kill other people, and never, ever say they are sorry, when they die they go to hell. Hell is a big fire and sounds pretty scary to me.

Sister Robert Julie says to always ask God for help. She said, God always listens and He will always help us even if it takes a long, long time. Sister says, never give up, God will always help us and if we try to do the right thing but don't always make it, if we ask, He will always forgive us and will never ever let anybody go to Hell who doesn't want to go.

I remember my Grandma, back in Wales, always asking God for strength. I'm pretty sure that when she looked up at the ceiling and said, "God give me strength," it was her way of asking God for help to do the right thing and keep herself and us, too, from going to Hell.

Mommy told me, because she goes to church, stays married to a man she hates, and takes care of us horrible children, it doesn't matter how much she yells and smacks us, because it is all our fault that she is in such a mess. Her God knows this because Mommy says she has told Him, and now He is mad at me, Billy, and the man who is our father.

I don't tell Mommy, but when she makes me kneel down and say my prayers, I only pray to Sister Robert Julie's God. I always remember what Sister Robert Julie says, that her God doesn't want anyone to go to Hell. I don't want me, Billy, Mommy or even the man who Mommy says is our father to go to Hell. I think of my Grandma looking up at the ceiling, and when Mommy's not looking, I do too. I ask Sister Robert Julie's God, and I'm pretty sure Grandma's God, to please give me strength against Mommy and her God always being mad at us.

I remember the man who Mommy says is our father, saying to Mommy, very quietly, after she hits the roof, "Well, excuse me for living!"

1946

BACK TO BEAUMARIS

Well, we're back in Beaumaris. We came on a great big ship that used to carry soldiers back and forth when the war was on. Mommy, Billy and I slept in bunk beds in a big cabin with lots of other women and children. Mommy was disgusted because she said we were like cows bunched up in a barn. She said it was not the way she was used to traveling.

When we came in the Lodge, Grandma was sitting by the fire. All of us were so happy to see her. She took Mommy in her arms and held on to her for dear life. Then she looked at us. Mommy said for us to stand back as we were so dirty from the train trip. Grandma smiled at us and said she was so happy we had come, but she wasn't feeling well and had better not kiss us. She said she didn't want us to get sick.

Grandma doesn't seem the same as when we were here before. Her eyes are not twinkling, and her hair has a lot more gray in it. Her voice is very soft... I can hardly hear what she says. She still has the little gold crosses in her ears. I remembered she always wore a black velvet ribbon around her throat, but it is gone.

She keeps smiling at us but she keeps holding Mommy's hands and won't let go. Grandpa is at work, but Grandma says he will be home at half-past five. Mommy says for Billy and me to go play outside as she wants to talk to Grandma alone. I whine. I want to stay with Grandma, but Mommy gives me her 'look' and I can see tears rolling down Grandma's cheeks. I know I better take Billy and go. Outside in the backyard I have tears in my eyes. I am such a cry baby.

The backyard looks so familiar. I go straight down to the bottom end of the garden and Billy goes to the other side of the yard.

One thing I remember, before we left for America, was Grandma taking my hand and walking me out of the house and leading me straight down to her special garden. Her eyes were twinkling and she had this huge smile on her face as she squeezed my hand and told me to look where she was pointing. She told me it was lilac. Grandma said to bend over and smell the lilac. I did. I remember laughing and laughing with Grandma as she said, "Aye child, the first time I smelled lilac I was as giddy as you!"' I'll never forget that day. It was as if Grandma was sharing with me, and only me, a wonderful secret.

The lilac bush is not in bloom now, but it makes me so happy it is still here in Grandma's garden that I cry some more.

It is so good to see Grandpa when he comes home from work. He picks each of us up and swings and twirls us around and around and as dirty as we are, he hugs us too. Mommy tells him to put us down or he will hurt his back, as he is too old and we are too big for such foolishness. Grandpa gives Mommy a funny look and says again he is so happy to see us. Then Mommy says for Billy and me to go outside, because she wants to talk to Grandpa alone. Grandpa says no, he'll talk to Mommy later. Right now he wants to talk to us, but first he wants Billy and me to help him take off his hobnail boots. He said nobody had helped him since we had gone to America.

Even being back with Grandma and Grandpa, Beaumaris gets worse by the day. After that first day, Grandma hardly comes out of her bedroom. Mommy says Grandma just needs an operation and she will be fine. Grandpa says no, she doesn't need an operation.

Mommy and Grandpa argue and argue. When Grandpa comes home from work he's always happy to see us but he goes straight up to Grandma's room. When he comes down the stairs, he eats something and then says he has to go out. Mommy's getting madder and madder because she says she knows where he's going—the pub!

I know if Mommy wants Grandma to have an operation, Grandma will have an operation.

The day Grandma went to the hospital it was just like most days in Beaumaris; it was freezing cold and big heavy clouds squashed all the color out of everything in sight. I said good-bye to Grandma and gave her a quick kiss on her cheek. I saw her stooped gray figure through the kitchen window panes as she disappeared with Mommy.

After they left, Billy and I walked down to our aunty and uncle's house on Margaret Street. We were to stay there until Mommy said for us to come back up to the lodge.

That night I slept with my cousin Shirley. She is seven years older than me. We slept in Shirley's room in a big double bed. In America, her room would be called the attic. It had a small square window that opened right out on top of the house. I had gotten out of bed and pushed it wide open. It seemed so very strange standing in front of that window, up there with the rooftops of Beaumaris, feeling the freezing cold air, then looking up and seeing a sliver of a moon. I was aware that the big squashy cloud that had been up in the sky all day (I think every day since we had been back in Beaumaris) had disappeared, and I could see lots and lots of twinkling stars.

Everything was so dark and still, except for Shirley crying softly into her pillow. I had begged her to tell me why she was crying, but she said I was too young to know. Standing at the wide open window and feeling so cold and hearing Shirley cry, I knew something had happened to Grandma.

When Mommy came to aunt and uncle's house the next day, she was furious. She told aunty that the doctor had killed Grandma. She said it was a simple operation and it was all the doctor's fault because he didn't know what he was doing.

They brought home a big wooden box. Mommy said it was Grandma. I snuck in the front parlor to see for myself. The room was dark, the curtains were pulled, and there were tall lit candles on either side of the long narrow box. I looked inside because the lid was up. I could see something that looked like my Grandma lying on a white satin sheet with the candlelight flickering on a stone-cold face. All it was, was a dressed-up gray statue that must have toppled over backwards and landed in this fancy box. My skin felt all prickly. Where was my real Grandma?

Mommy has put Billy and me in school. Billy is in the primary school, the same as kindergarten, but I think, much different. I am put in the first form. I would have been in second grade in Salinas. Nothing is the same as Salinas. The teacher told Mommy that I am very slow and it is very unfortunate I can't speak a word of Welsh. I am homesick for my friend Joan, warm rooms, electric lights, telephones, Sacred Heart School, and Sister Robert Julie. Most of all, I miss an indoor bathroom.

Grandpa is so mad at Mommy he still won't talk to her. He never comes home in time to see us anymore.

School is the worst. The teachers are very strict, much more strict than Sister Robert Julie. I feel really sorry for Billy not getting to go to Kindergarten in Salinas.

Then I met my friend Gwyneth. The day didn't start out so good; it was the day I got caught talking in school. The teacher called me up to his desk and told me to put my right hand out. Without taking his eyes off me he raised from his desk drawer his special ruler. He brought it down hard across the palm of my hand. The smack made me jump and, of course, brought tears to my eyes. It wasn't that bad, but I could hear the boys laughing behind me. I was so ashamed. I was told to go back to my desk and if I talked again, I would get the cane.

After school, Gwyneth, the cleverest girl in my class, the girl who all the teachers in the whole school knew, the girl who had the prettiest honey-colored hair and spoke Welsh perfectly, came up to me and said, "I thought you were very brave. Never mind, nobody cares tuppence for old beak nose. Do you want to walk home with me? I live just up the hill from the Lodge."

"Sure."

"You have a very queer accent. But I think it's smashing. What's America like?"

"I liked it, but they think I talk funny too."

"Right, come on let's you and me be friends!"

Beginning that day and everyday after school, we'd find each other and walk home together. We'd walk and walk and talk and talk. Gwyneth loves the movies, only she calls them the picture shows.

"Have you ever been to Hollywood, Marion?"

"Gosh no, shall we go when we're all grown-up? Sister Robert Julie told me that

Salinas is in California and she told me that Hollywood is in California, so I'll take you there."

"That would be ever so super. My dear, whatever shall we wear?"

"Do you prefer satin or taffeta?"

"Either, but you do realize our dresses simply must be strapless—and of course, we will wear our hair up with double-diamond tiaras and gobs and gobs of red lipstick."

"Of course, Your Royal Highness."

One day, Gwyneth and I were walking home pretending to be famous movie stars when a few drops of rain splashed on our faces. We looked at each other and we just started running.

Gwyneth yelled through the rain that we were cowboys and we had to save a maverick at the top of the hill.

"Yippee, lets go!"

We ran up the hill holding on to our pretend reins all the way. Then the rain really came down. The harder it rained, the faster we ran. We turned our horses around and galloped down the hill. The rain kept coming, and we were laughing hysterically as we got off our horses, stomping and sloshing through the instant puddles.

The shower stopped as quickly as it started. Gwyneth and I didn't care, because we were worried there might be Indians behind the tree. It wasn't Indians; it was Mommy who came up behind us. I felt the stinging smack on my bottom and bare legs.

She shouted, "How stew-pit can the two of you be? Gwyneth Paynter, I thought *you* had more sense. Get home, both of you!"

She grabbed my hand and pulled me up the hill. Gwyneth had run ahead of us and as Mommy and I turned into Grandma's house, Gwyneth shouted back to me, "Marion, don't forget tomorrow is Saturday; we're going to the picture show."

My mother shouted back, "I'm afraid Marion won't be going anywhere tomorrow, Gwyneth!"

Inside Grandma's house, Mommy pulled me over to the fire and, as she took my wet clothes off, she started in. "It will serve you right if you catch your death, acting like a foolish tomboy!"

The next day, because I couldn't go to the movie with Gwyneth, she went with her cousin to the next town over, Menai Bridge.

Sunday we heard in church that Gwyneth had been killed in Menai Bridge. She was having tea with her cousin when Gwyneth needed to go to the bathroom. Her cousin also had Gwyneth's little brother with her, so she told Gwyneth to go quickly across the street as there was no inside bathroom in the tea shop. Crossing the street, Gwyneth was run over by a lady trying to park her new car.

The day of her funeral, the whole first form from school went to the cemetery. Each of us dropped tiny bluebells and snowdrops down into the hole where they put Gwyneth. Just like my Grandma, none of us will ever see Gwyneth again.

 **1947**

LEWIS' COFFEE SHOP

About a month after Gwyneth died, my mother booked second-class passage on the Queen Elizabeth for the three of us to go back to Salinas, California, to be with our father. When she decided, or how she got the money, I never knew.

As we came into port, I was looking out a small round porthole. The ship passed a beautiful statue of a lady standing almost in the water. I knew she was standing there welcoming my mother, Billy and me. Seeing the Statue of Liberty, I was thrilled to be back in America.

In Salinas, Mom told me that, if anybody asked what my father did, I was to say, "He is retired." I'm not sure I actually knew what the word "retired" meant. I did know he worked in the back room of a saloon as a card dealer when we were in Salinas before. Mom said I was never to tell anyone that.

This time, back in Salinas, Mom told him he was to quit working in the back room of saloons and open a restaurant. Mom rented a house and charmed the owner into remodeling the downstairs into "Lewis' Coffee Shop."

She hit on what she thought was a million-dollar idea: fish and chips. In 1947, in Salinas, the men working in the truck and fertilizer plant next door, in the tractor company across the street, and in the Coca Cola bottling company up the street, were not interested in fish and chips. They wanted hamburger steak with onions and french fries (Don't call them chips!), chicken fried steak with onions and fries, chili with onions and fries, strong black coffee, glazed and jam filled donuts, snails and bear claws. When the coffee shop first opened, it was summer and I would help serve in the early morning. I always waited for one of the men to ask for a snail with french fries! Nobody did.

At first, my father really enjoyed the coffee shop. He made Farmer Brothers coffee in the big silver urns and bantered with the men. The coffee shop was a great success. Mom learned to make chili and chicken fried steak with gravy. She was a big hit with the customers. She had a very British accent, and she joked and told stories.

I remember the day Mom decided she hated the coffee shop and cooking. She was in the restaurant behind the counter, laughing and talking to two men from the tractor company across the street. She jokingly asked how old did they think she was? The big burly guy, who everyone called Greenfield, said he didn't know—

maybe forty? The other guy, tall and blond, said he thought more like forty-five, forty-six? That did it. Mom stomped back in the kitchen, threw the dish towel down, turned on the gas burner, threw the hamburgers in the frying pan and went upstairs to bed! When the kitchen filled with smoke, my father and I ran in, trying to save whatever was burning in the pan. He was as helpless in the kitchen as I was. When my mother finally came down the stairs, she announced she was through working in a place that made her old before her time. She was thirty-nine.

After that, customers stopped coming, and my father started getting hold of me. I was nine, turning ten. The first time it was on the stairs off the kitchen. There were no customers in the shop. He came out of the kitchen as I was going up the stairs. When he grabbed me, I thought he was playing, as lately he had been really nice to me but when I turned towards him, he put his lips on mine and stuck his tongue into my mouth. It surprised me so much that I thought I would vomit. Someone must have come into the coffee shop because he left as quickly as he appeared. I wiped my mouth in disbelief. Why had he done that? I hated it.

He caught me several more times. The last time, I pushed him as hard as I could and said,

"Please don't do that." He didn't say a word, he just went back to cleaning the countertop.

I started avoiding him. I kept on the other side of the counter. I made sure I knew where he was before I went down the second hallway off the kitchen or up the stairs.

Telling Mom was out of the question. These days, every time she looked at me she ranted and raved over something I had done or hadn't done. I knew that what my father was doing was wrong. I also knew my mother would never take my side. She would say it was my fault. No, I would not tell my mother. I would just stay away from him. He didn't scare me.

One day I needed fifty-cents for school. Mom said, "Ask your father!" and then went upstairs. I shouted to him from the kitchen if I could have two quarters for school. He said yes, but I had to come and take it from the cash register myself. There had been no customers in the shop all morning, so I was pretty sure I knew what that meant. I really needed the fifty-cents for the pagan babies because there was a contest at school to see which class could collect the most money. I figured, okay, I'll keep my lips tightly together and move fast.

Knowing what I knew, I still went down the length of the counter to the cash register. He didn't try to kiss me, but his hands were all over me! I let him touch me as I hit the key on the cash register. The red tag, NO SALE, flipped up and the till slid open. I grabbed two quarters, slammed the till shut, and bolted away!

Outside, I again felt like vomiting as I felt the two quarters in my hand. How could I have done that? I did something bad for money!

All the way back to school I knew I was going to Hell. As I put the money in the collection box, I promised God I would go to confession. I was sick to my stomach for days.

Every Friday afternoon, Sister (it was not Sister Robert Julie) would march us over to the church so the whole school could go to confession. Sister said Father's time was very limited, "So be quick and don't dawdle." My stomach was in knots. I wanted to go to confession, but I was scared to death. As it got closer and closer to my turn, I was panicking. What would I say? I knew I had done wrong, but I didn't know how I was going to confess to Father. Finally, when I was kneeling in the confessional, I said as fast as I could, "Bless me Father, for I have sinned, I took fifty-cents from my father's cash register and that's all I can think of."

The priest said for my penance I needed to earn fifty cents and give it back to my father *in his hands* and tell him I was sorry for stealing from him. I must say the Act of Contrition and tell God I will never steal again. "Go in peace, my child, and sin no more. Please send the next child in." I came out of the confessional feeling worse than when I went in. What was I going to do?

I knew I didn't want to go anywhere near my father. I was never, never going to do what I did again, so help me God.

It was at that moment I 'heard' what I had to do to get myself out of this mess. I didn't know where the voice came from, but I knew I would do what it said.

Okay, Marion, this is what you are going to do. First, forget the fifty-cents. God will just have to understand. Second, promise God you will never go near that cash register or your father ever again. Third, don't tell anybody. The only way this could be worse for you is if your mother finds out. Ask God to forgive you and if Mom's God sends you to Hell, at least you know you can trust Sister Robert Julie's God; he won't tell your mother!

I did what the voice said, and I had no more problems with my father. I never spoke to him directly or went near him. Nobody noticed.

Mom was becoming more and more frustrated with my father and us children. Both Billy and I learned to just stay out of her way as much as possible. It was easier for Billy, being the boy. Mom never told him to do any housework. He was free to go and come as he pleased. Mom had a job for me every time she caught sight of me.

One day, I had just finished washing and drying the dishes and started running up the stairs. Mom came in the kitchen and yelled at me to come back into the kitchen. The stairs were right off the kitchen, and I was already halfway up the stairs. I stopped, turned around, and yelled, "Now what?"

Mom came to the bottom of the stairs, looked up at me and yelled, "Don't you dare answer me back or use that tone with me, young lady. Get down here this minute! Did you think you can get away with your sluttish ways by putting a broken cup in the cupboard and I wouldn't notice?"

I stood fast on the stairs. "What broken cup? I didn't put a broken cup in the cupboard."

"You impudent hussy; I won't tolerate my own daughter bare face lying to me!"

Mom came right up the stairs and slapped me hard across the face.

"I'll teach you to lie and answer me back!"

I looked at her and said, "Mom, this is so crazy, why are you doing this?"

"Shut up, you little lying slut! I'm your mother and I'll teach you to answer me back!" She slapped me again and again until blood poured out of my nose. I put my hand to my face to stop the blood. When Mom saw the blood she looked really frightened, backed down the stairs and started crying. "Mom, don't cry, I'm sorry, but I didn't break a cup!"

My mother shouted, "Look what you made me do! Get out of my sight, you good-for-nothing lying slut!"

I had never made my mother cry before. She was always the one to make me cry. Her crying scared me.

Why won't my mother ever believe me? I didn't break a cup...did I? Oh God, if there is a broken cup in the cupboard I honestly didn't see it. No matter what I do or say, my mother thinks I'm a lying slut. Sister Julie's God, please, please help me, I do not want to be a lying slut.

A few days later I was on the stairs, this time coming down. Mom yelled from the kitchen, "Marion, get down here this minute!"

I instantly stopped and thought, "Oh God, here we go again. Okay God, Blessed Mother, give me strength!" I walked down the rest of the stairs and into the kitchen.

"How many times have I told you to not leave your dirty dishes on the table, slut! Look at this mess!" I took the dirty dishes to the sink and started washing and drying them. They were not mine. I had been down in the bathroom getting ready for my friend's mother to pick me up. I had not been in the kitchen all morning. It was Saturday and my friend, Joan, and her mother were going shopping, and they had invited me to go with them. I knew Mom was already angry that I was going off with my friend, and she was stuck in the coffee shop. That voice inside me said, *Marion, don't say a word—just wash the dishes.*

Please, dear God, I don't want another repeat of what happened a few days ago on the stairs. A year and a half ago, it had all started on the same stairs with my father. Thank you, Sister Julie's God, for helping me keep away from my father.

Mom makes up her mind what the truth is and nothing I say or do will change her mind. Please, Sister Julie's God, help me not make things worse by opening my mouth in front of my mother. Please God help me to keep peace by not arguing. But God, I don't believe a word my mother says!

ART ON THE CEILING

One day, when I was eleven, I came home from school late in the afternoon. As I walked in the door, I saw my father slumped down on his stool by the cash register with his face as white as his hair. He spoke to me, one of the few times ever. He said, "Can you help in the kitchen?"

I knew something bad must have happened. I had a terrible feeling in my stomach as I walked down the length of the coffee counter; all I could think was, "Oh God, give me strength."

Not a customer sat in the place and the empty silence was terrifying. Usually when I got home from school, Mom would be in the kitchen yelling at my father or banging and throwing pots and pans around. I remember it was the silence that made me so sick to my stomach as I walked in the kitchen.

The kitchen was a disaster, much worse than usual: the sink piled high with dirty dishes, the pressure cooker in the middle of the stove on its side, and its lid in the middle of the floor.

Then I saw the ceiling, and nearly dropped my school books as I started laughing out loud.

My stomach instantly settled down. It was so beautiful! Individual red kidney beans hung on end, making a near perfect ring around a precisely outlined, circular splattered glob of ground beef and sauce. Dark tomato red against chalk white. An upside-down, three dimensional, delightful picture on the kitchen ceiling! I loved it.

My mother came down the stairs yelling, "You think it's so funny, *you* clean it up!"

Standing on the stove to reach the beans, it was a horrible mess rather than a beautiful work of art—but I still couldn't stop smiling.

I understood what happened: Mom got mad at something or other, went upstairs and forgot the pressure cooker. It retaliated by throwing up all its contents onto the ceiling. The result was strange, funny, beautiful, and, after the fact, harmless.

Somewhere down deep I had the feeling, is this my mother? Can I just laugh?

MY COUSIN, DOROTHY

My father had a great niece, Dorothy, living in England. She had served in the British Army for nine years. She was unmarried and had no ties. Mom thought Dorothy could come to America and cook in the coffee shop, so she wrote to Dorothy and invited her to come and live with us.

Dorothy came to Salinas in 1950, but she had no intention of cooking for no wages. She immediately found a good-paying job with Montgomery Ward. This made Mom so mad that she got Dorothy to help her get a job with Montgomery Ward too. Mom left my father high and dry in the coffee shop. I was spending more and more time at school and with my friends. I avoided the coffee shop at all costs.

Dorothy worked in the cashier's office of Montgomery Ward and my mother worked in the credit department. In the beginning, Dorothy and my mother walked to work together, ate lunch together, and walked home together.

Mom's job was skip-tracing 'bums' who had skipped out on paying their bill. Mom said that no one could escape her. I knew she was right.

When Dorothy got home, she was always helpful around the house. She and I would do the dishes after dinner and talk. I liked her; she was the closest thing I had to a sister even though she was eighteen years older than me. After dinner, Dorothy would make the sofa bed up in the dining room and go to bed.

When Billy and I went upstairs to bed, Mom would come up and tell us we were not to listen to Dorothy.. I don't remember Billy being so interested, but Dorothy had been in the Women's British Army for nine years, and I wanted to listen to her stories of what it was like during the war. Mom said it was all hooey, and she forbade both Billy and me to listen to anything Dorothy had to say. Billy didn't care one way or the other. He had pretty much stopped listening or talking to any of us. He went to school and did his own thing. To keep peace, I knew I needed to stay away from Dorothy around my mother.

Then my father had a heart attack. A few months later he was diagnosed with cancer and was very sick. Mom closed the coffee shop and moved us all to a huge white elephant of a house on Central Avenue. Mom rented out the extra bedrooms. Dorothy moved to the big house with us and paid rent to Mom for the bedroom she now shared with me. If Mom heard me talking to

Dorothy in our bedroom she would always tell me to turn my light off and go to sleep.

Not long after we moved to the big house, my father died, and my mother fell hard for Fred. Fred rented one of the rooms in our house. Mom didn't cook for any of the other renters, but she did cook for Fred, especially on the weekends. Fred was gay, but no one ever used that word then. There was no word we used; we just all knew Fred was different. Mom really liked Fred and she said if anyone could change Fred's mind, she could. We all genuinely liked Fred. Fred was a good person and a good friend. Mom was completely different around him. I think Fred was the only person my mother ever thought she loved.

The big house was a fantastic old Victorian, but had been neglected for years. The owners had moved out of town and were unable to sell it. About a year after my father died, Fred moved out to an apartment. Mom decided she'd had enough of the rundown rooming house. Mom, Dorothy, Billy and I moved across the street to a small house on Stone Street. Billy's room was way in the back; he had his own private entrance.

One day I came home to find Mom yelling hysterically at Dorothy. This was a first; Mom had never confronted Dorothy face-to-face before. I came in the house just as Mom was screaming her head off that she had seen Dorothy make eyes at Fred! Make eyes at Fred? What in the world was she talking about? My mom was standing in her bedroom and shouting through the two open doors of the bathroom between her bedroom and Dorothy's and my bedroom.

"Don't think I don't know what's going on. You can just pack your bags and get out. I'm sick of you carrying on with Fred behind my back."

Dorothy was dumbfounded and kept saying, "Molly, I don't know what you're talking about."

My mother wasn't listening; she just kept shouting over anything Dorothy tried to say. Mom's voice got even louder, "I said pack your bags and get out of my house!"

I can't describe how angry I became as it dawned on me what Mom was saying. Dorothy had been with us since before my father died. She'd gotten Mom a job with her at Montgomery Ward and she paid Mom rent every week. She never made trouble and she had no other family in America. Where was she supposed to go? This was really idiotic of my mother.

I remembered Grandma saying, "Something inside me snapped!" That's exactly what happened to me. I lost my temper. I marched into our bedroom past Dorothy and stood in the bathroom between the two bedrooms and, for the first time since Mom had made my nose bleed, I let my mother have it.

"For God's sake, Mom. This is the stupidest thing I've ever heard. Who in the hell cares if Dorothy did make eyes at Fred?"

Dorothy came into the bathroom and put her hand on my right arm and said, "Honestly Marion, I didn't...."

Mom hit the roof. She grabbed my left arm and pushed me aside, "Get out of the way— traitor! You know nothing and it's none of your business! And for your information, the word is stew-pit not stoo-pid, stew-pit. Don't you dare say 'Hell' in front of me, young lady. Now stew-pit, hold your tongue, before I knock the living daylights out of you!"

I stood my ground and said, "Right, hit me because you think Dorothy made eyes at Fred? Is that what a good Catholic is taught to do?"

Mom was so furious with what I said that she sizzled. She yanked my arm, making me lose my balance. "How dare you say such a thing to me, your mother!"

Dorothy got hold of my other arm and pulled me back on my two feet. "Molly, don't."

My mother pulled with both hands so hard that I fell on my knees. "She's my daughter; don't touch her!"

Dorothy helped me get up as Mom momentarily gathered momentum. Dorothy started to pull me toward our bedroom as she said, "Molly, be reasonable."

Mom screamed as she got hold of my other arm, "She's *my* daughter; I'm calling the police!"

With my mother and Dorothy pulling me in two different directions, I screamed at the top of my lungs, *"Why am I living with crazy people?"*

Both of them instantly let go of my arms. My mother stood frozen with her eyebrows reaching for the ceiling, her unblinking eyes black with rage, and her mouth pulled tight. Dorothy was also motionless with both arms limp at her sides, a look of total confusion on her face.

Good, I shut them both up, was all I could think as I ran from the now silent house.

It was Saturday afternoon and Sacred Heart church was half a block away. I ran into the church. One person was waiting to go into confession. I got in line. Before I knew it, I was kneeling in the confessional.

"Bless me, Father, for I have sinned—I just had a terrible fight with my mother."

"I see, go on child."

"My mother is kicking Dorothy out of the house"

"I see. Who is Dorothy, your sister?"

"No, she's—well, she's my father's brother's granddaughter? No, that's not right. Oh Father, I don't know who she is! She's a relative on my father's side from Wales, like we are, and Mom wrote to her and asked her to come live with us. She's been with us a long time. She got my mom a job and she pays Mom rent. Mom is really mad because she says Dorothy made eyes at Fred."

"I see. Who is Fred?"

"Fred is this really nice man who used to rent a room from us when we lived in the big house. But my mother made such a fuss over him, he moved out. I know my mother has fallen for Fred. But Fred, well, Fred isn't interested. Fred is, well, he's really nice and he's a good friend to all of us, and we all know he just wants to be a friend. Dorothy would never make eyes at Fred; she has a boyfriend."

"I see. So is Fred making eyes at Dorothy?"

"No, no—my mother said Dorothy made eyes at Fred."

"I see. Why did your mother say that?"

"That's it, Father. That's why I'm so mad: I don't know. My mother is always saying crazy untrue things to me, but she's never outright accused Dorothy before. What gives my mother the right to say Dorothy can't make eyes at Fred? Nobody's married."

"I see. Your mother is not married? Is Fred your father?"

"No! Of course not. Oh Father, forget it. You couldn't possibly understand—nobody can." I got up and left.

I walked straight down the aisle and plunked myself down in the corner, by the side chapel of the Blessed Mother in the very front of the church. It was dark and cool. I had to have time to think. As I sat there I began realizing that I had actually yelled at my mother and I had walked out on the priest in the confessional!

I had never done anything like this before, and I felt bad. Still, I kept seeing Dorothy's and my mother's faces as I ran from the house. I kept hearing the priest say, "I see." I took a huge breath and as I leaned against the wood bench, tears poured down my face, but I was laughing! I realized the whole thing was so silly, so stupid. Dorothy's a big girl; she can take care of herself and I cannot let myself be drawn into my mother's illogical ideas! Oh God, please, please, *give me strength*!

After a few minutes, as I wiped my face with my sleeve, I became aware of the candles twinkling in the semidarkness: row after row of candles burning in front of the statue of Our Lady. I looked up at the beautiful white alabaster statue of Mary in the soft candlelight, with her eyes looking straight at me, her arms outstretched, and in my whole being I could feel she was laughing with me! At that moment, I knew exactly what my grandmother would say: "Marion, it's a sign! It's a sign from God!"

I took another deep breath and said, "Oh Blessed Mother, what is wrong with my mother? What goes on in her head to make her think and say such untrue things? You know she'll never say she was wrong. I bet Dorothy's wondering if she *did* make eyes at Fred?"

I began to think of my grandmother, how many times did I hear her asking God, the Blessed Mother, all the Saints, for strength dealing with my mother? I am in the same boat as my Grandma!

Suddenly I had this incredible feeling that Grandma was sitting right next to me and both the Blessed Mother and she were telling me, "Marion, we don't know what to do with Molly, either. Just keep asking God for strength and laugh, Marion, laugh! Oh, and *never, never,* make eyes at Fred!"

MRS. JOHNSON

In 1956, I graduated from high school and was scared out of my mind. What was I to do next?

Mrs. Johnson, a lady I had been babysitting for, asked me if I would like to come and live with her and be a mother's helper. She said I could attend Hartnell, the junior college, about two blocks from her house. Mom said that was the most ridiculous idea she'd ever heard! I was to get a proper job with Montgomery Ward and start paying her back for all the money she'd forked out for me. I was stupid if all I wanted to do was be someone's skivvy!

Skivvy? Slut? Hussy? How, why, does my mother come up with these names to call me? I had to look up the word "skivvy" in the dictionary. It's a British word most often used meaning a servant of the most menial tasks. It's the word that gave me the courage to make a decision. I decided I would rather be a "skivvy" than live in my mother's house and work for Montgomery Ward.

Mom was so mad she wouldn't let me take any of my clothes from the house. I ended up sliding in and out a bathroom window to get what I needed.

I felt a whole new world had opened up for me. Mrs. Johnson taught me to cook, clean, and take care of babies; but she said that going to college was more important for me in the long run.

After I got my drivers license, Mrs. Johnson let me take her car to the grocery store. (My mother sold my deceased father's car the day I turned sixteen because she said she would never trust me to drive.) After I had been driving for a while, Mrs. Johnson trusted me to take the children where they need to go after school. I never forgot how much Mrs. Johnson's trust in me meant.

Mrs. Johnson knew how much I loved acting. She encouraged me to try out for the Little Theatre's production of *The Merchant of Venice*. I got the part of Portia. It was the highlight of my whole life in 1957. Such an amazing play. I couldn't believe my good fortune to study an outstanding play by William Shakespeare and be given the opportunity to be Portia, an intelligent woman!

Mr. Ulrici, our director, made all of us think and talk about the dark undertow of bigotry in the play. I felt Shylock's pain when he went on and on about the cruelty he had endured from people who said they were Christians!

In this play, Shakespeare succinctly put the point across that as human beings we are all flawed, and in the same boat—Catholics, Protestants, Jews, Muslims, men, women, mothers and daughters. Chuck and I discussed the play endlessly.

Meeting Chuck was a bolt from behind! It was my first college dance and my friend's mom had given me her prize dance dress from when she was in college. It was a strapless, fire-engine red taffeta with black lace inserts. Mrs. Johnson helped me take up the hem so it was waltz-length and I wore several puffy petticoats underneath. I love to dance and had been practicing and practicing in the Johnson's living room with Mary, the Johnson's ten year old daughter.

At the dance, I was jitterbugging with my partner when he spun me out and I went reeling into something that sent me smack to the floor! Stars is not what I saw as I hit the ground. I saw red taffeta and petticoats flying every which way, and I wanted to keep going right through the floor!

Suddenly, someone was standing over me, apologizing like crazy, saying it was his fault; and as I pushed all that taffeta and organza off my eyes, I realized everyone had stopped dancing and the guy apologizing was Chuck Besmehn! I knew who he was. My best friend from first grade, Joan, who turned out to be one of the cutest girls in our class, had dated him in high school. Now, I really wanted to die. The boy I had been dancing with and Chuck both helped me and my myriad of red taffeta and petticoats get up off the floor. I was so embarrassed that Sandy, my friend, said my face turned the exact color of my dress! I left the dance after that.

Chuck found out where I was living and called the Johnson's the next day. He talked to Mrs. Johnson and told her he was the cause of my accident at the dance last night. He wanted to know if I was okay? She said she didn't know that I had had an accident, but suggested that he come over and see for himself, if he were so concerned.

Both Mr. and Mrs. Johnson liked Chuck—an Engineering student planning to transfer to Cal Berkeley the following semester. I was going to miss him. I really, really liked him. When I got the lead in the play, Chuck made a deal with me and the Johnson's, saying he would study in the library until rehearsals were over, then he'd bring me home. Lots of nights he'd come to rehearsal a half hour early and watch. On the way home, we'd discuss the play and how it was going.

He could always start me laughing. Like I said, the Johnson's really liked him, but gave him a hard time because he wasn't Catholic. He claimed that the Presbyterians had the best and most available gym in Salinas and until the Catholics or any other denomination could come up with better facilities, he'd stick with being a Presbyterian. I don't know why, but it made me laugh and made the Johnson's roll their eyes. I began to understand and appreciate his irreverent sense of humor and his undramatic, perfectly logical solutions to problems—mine or his.

I remember thinking, "Is it possible that life can be this good? Are Mrs. Johnson and Chuck the kind of people I can have in my life? Grandma, I'm giddy! It's as if I'm smelling the lilacs you showed me in your garden."

1958

MOLLY GOES TO HOLLYWOOD

In 1958, Mom wrote to Jack Bailey, the host of the popular television show, *Queen for a Day*. Her letter was so compelling that she was sent a ticket to fly to Hollywood and compete in the final round. If she won, she would become a contestant on the show. The contestants with the saddest sob story won by applause and would appear on the show. Whoever won on the show itself was crowned Queen for a Day and given the royal treatment, with lots and lots of prizes to make up for the *Queen's* horrible, unfortunate, and terrible life.

Mrs. Johnson said I could borrow her car to take Mom to the Salinas airport. Dorothy came with me and we saw her off. I was so impressed: Mom flying for the very first time, in a small plane with two other passengers, not at all nervous. I remember thinking I would be scared to death to fly for the very first time by myself and then be a contestant on TV. Mom was raring to go and just knew she would be Queen for a Day. I loved seeing Mom so excited and happy. She said she was bound to win as no one could possibly have a sadder life story than she.

How many times had I heard versions of her sob story before and since?

"I came to this country a young bride, completely alone with no family. There was talk of war and I was so worried about my parents. I promised my husband, if I could just once more go back to Wales to see my mother and father, I would come back to America for the birth of the baby I was carrying.

"But war broke out while my fourteen-month-old daughter, my unborn child and I were on the Atlantic Ocean, trying to reach my aging parents. The ship ahead of us and the ship behind us were both torpedoed. With great hardship, I finally reached my parents' home.

"Because of the war, I was not able to come back to America. Our son was born with bombs bursting all around us in Wales. It was the son my husband had always prayed for. My husband's greatest wish was to see his only son before he died.

"When my son was three years old, we were finally allowed to secretly leave England during the middle of the war. We were the only passengers on a small ship surrounded by a convoy of warships. We spent a harrowing six weeks zigzagging across the North Atlantic under constant threat of German U-Boats and German aeroplanes. We were never allowed to take our clothes off—or remove our lifejackets. We lived day and night with the constant ear-shattering sound of the emergency siren and emergency drills, and the ships all around us had their guns exploding. I was a nervous wreck for the safety of my two children. In the month we were at sea, there was not a moment of peace.

"My husband moved Heaven and Earth and used all his resources to obtain passage for us. For the six weeks we were at sea, he did not know if we were alive or dead.

"I was able to keep my promise and present his son safely to him. When we finally arrived, he had aged overnight and was very sick. He saw his son, but he died soon after. He left me penniless, homeless and with two children who I've raised completely alone, having no family to turn to in this country."

Mom flew back from Los Angeles furious because she wasn't even a contestant on live TV! Before the show my mother and another lady were vying to be the last contestant on TV with Jack Bailey. The audience picked the other lady by the applause meter, just before the show began.

The other lady was a widow with eight children, and she was in a wheelchair. Mom talked about this woman for years, saying, "All the applause went to the stew-pit widow in a bloody wheelchair! She didn't even need it. I saw her stand before we went on stage. The wheelchair was just a gimmick. I could kick myself for not thinking of it!"

1959

ARROYO SECO

Today is unimaginable. The sunlight bouncing on the water dazzles my eyes. I have been in the clear cold river, but now I've climbed out to sit on this huge rock in the warm sun to see if I can make any sense of what is happening to me. I wonder if this strange delicious fog that has crept inside my brain will lift?

This morning I had left for school in plenty of time for my first class, but I never made it. I ran into my friend, Sandy, from high school. She said her boyfriend, John, and my boyfriend, Chuck, wanted to take us swimming in Arroyo Seco. So instead of going to my first class, I'd gone back to the Johnson's, the family I'm living with, grabbed my bathing suit and a towel, told Mrs. Johnson I'd be home in time to babysit this evening, and left.

My friends picked me up outside the house and we took off in John's new Chevy.

So now, here we are in Arroyo Seco, high in the foothills that stretch all down the western side of the Salinas Valley. At least fifty miles from Hartnell College, where I'm supposed to be.

What am I thinking? Sandy and John are nowhere in sight. Chuck is swimming in long slow strides back and forth across the river. I love watching him. He's a strong, powerful swimmer. I am not. I can swim, barely. I always keep my head above water because I'm deathly afraid of going under. My mother says I'm afraid of my own shadow. Which is mostly true. But today I'm not afraid of the water: I'm with Chuck.

The river here is not wide, but deep and peaceful. The silence is breathtaking. I have no idea which path we took to get to this particular spot. Never in my life have I done anything like this. The nuns would say, "Marion, you are just asking for trouble."

My mother would say, "How stew-pit can you be; haven't I always said you were a slut?"

Am I a slut? I am overcome with this persistent, delicious fog that's overtaking my head, my heart, my whole being! Whatever I am, whatever I'm feeling, I know this is my decision to be here. I am in this beautiful isolated place with someone I really like because I want to be. I could stay forever!

He's swimming back to me. He's treading water and splashing me. I'm splashing back. He's pulling my foot.

"Oh Chuck, don't scare me; the water's too deep."

My foot is free, but now he's hoisting himself onto my rock, and I'm in his arms! Oh my gosh—he's kissing me! Oh wow, I'm kissing *him!* I'm really kissing him! I hear a voice...his. "We need to go. I love you!"

We're slipping, sliding....

Oh, my God! This water is freezing!

The fog is gone! Coughing, choking, gasping...again I hear,"Do you think you can swim straight across the river? I've got to get you back in time to babysit. I promise not to let you go under!"

PART III

MY MOLLY PROBLEM

 **1986**

CASA SERENA

After my marriage to Chuck in 1960, he takes his first engineering job with Bechtel, a big construction company out of San Francisco. By 1971 we have three sons. Chuck's job requires we start moving to different places in the U.S. and Canada.

In 1975, we head across the Pacific to Jakarta, Indonesia. Chuck loves his work and the farther from my mom, the better for me.

My husband, the boys and I are in Indonesia a total of five years. Not only in Jakarta, on the Island of Java, but also Lhokseumawe, on the Island of Sumatra.

The two older boys finish high school. The youngest, in eighth grade, begs to come home until he finishes high school.

We come home to San Francisco. But Chuck has to go to Alaska. Paul and I stay in San Francisco. Paul is a sophomore in high school when I get the phone call from Dorothy.

Mom has had a stroke. She is in the hospital; Dorothy wants to know, can I come?

By the time I get to Salinas from San Francisco, she is stabilized. I spend the night in the hospital. Mom is sleeping comfortably. The next day they transfer Molly to Casa Serena, a high skilled nursing home. I am told the stroke affected her right side. Nothing is wrong with her mind or her speech.

I come into her room in Casa Serena. She says to me immediately, "You're the one who's responsible for this! God will pay you back, Missy. Don't think he won't."

"Mom, you had a stroke. Dorothy called me at home."

"Home? You don't have a home. Your place is here, taking care of me."

The nurse comes in and says, "OK, Mrs. Lewis, I'm going to get you up so your daughter can take you for a nice ride in the wheelchair. You're doing just fine. If you keep up the good work, your daughter will be able to take you home with her in a day or two."

As the nurse helps my mother up and into the wheelchair, the nurse looks at me and says, "Your mom is so sweet. Don't worry, she'll be home in no time. Just take her for a quick spin, then leave her in the room at the end of the hall for physical therapy. Tomorrow, Mrs. Lewis, you'll be even better than today."

"Thank you, nurse. Will I be able to play golf tomorrow?"

"Oh, Mrs. Lewis, I think that will take a little longer."

Mom gives the nurse a lopsided smile and says, "I certainly hope whatever you're doing to me improves my golf stroke—especially since I've never played golf or had a stroke before in my life!"

The nurse chuckles as she leaves the room saying, "Oh, Mrs. Lewis, you are such a character; I wish all the patients had your sense of humor."

I get behind the wheelchair. As I push my mother down the hall, she says in a whisper, "Marion, tomorrow I'm going home. I've already called my social worker; he said I can bring you up on elder abuse. Don't think I won't make you pay. God is on my side, Missy!"

I leave Casa Serena thinking, "Well she's certainly her old self. God knows what she has told that social worker!"

I sleep in my mother's room in her apartment for the second night. I'm awake for hours, plotting how I can disappear from Salinas. But eventually I think, "Marion, be serious, your poor mother has had a stroke; this may very well be the end."

I've always wanted my mother to be safe, healthy, and happy. Long ago, though, I gave up the idea of wanting anything from her for myself. Still, near dawn, facing the possibility of her death, I realize that there's one thing I desperately want from her.

The next day, I ask the nurse if I can take my mother outside to the magnolia tree that I'd discovered in a tiny neglected garden, just around the back of Casa Serena. The day is sunny and warm. Not always a possibility in a Salinas summer, known for thick, gray fog scooting up the valley from the Pacific Ocean, along with wind that can slice you in two. Not unlike my mother, slicing me in two with her tongue.

The small magnolia tree is in full bloom with huge white, waxy flowers. Mom is very quiet and hasn't said a word since I brought her outside. I stop at a small round metal table, put the brake on the wheelchair and sit in one of two rusted chairs opposite my mother. Suddenly, with aggravation in her voice that I know so well, she says, "Marion, why in hell am I here?"

"Mom, you had a stroke."

"Oh, don't be stew-pit, I know I had a stroke; why have you brought me to this miserable excuse for a garden? When are you taking me home?"

"Mom, I thought we could talk—I didn't sleep a wink last night thinking about you and me. I know I'm nothing like you wanted me to be, but Mom, I do love you and I have never in my life wanted anything bad to happen to you. I want more than anything in the world for you and I, just this once, to connect—now, more than ever..."

"*Connect*? What rot! Don't try to pussyfoot around me, after what you've done and are doing to your mother!"

"Mom, look in my eyes and tell me, what is wrong with me?"

She looks right at me. "Your hair. How many times have I told you, your hair is a mess!"

"OK," I laugh, "I'll fix my hair, Mom. But can't we talk about us? Do you really think I have been a terrible daughter?"

"Yes, I do. You abandoned me, your own mother, to this hell hole. Your father lied to me, your brother is too busy to come and see me, and you have forsaken me! You are my daughter —I blame you the most! Your brother has a family to take care of. God knows, I have no one!"

"Mom, that's not true. I've always kept in touch with you. Chuck and I help as much as we can. I've been more available since we moved back to San Francisco and Dorothy's come back from retiring in England to live with you."

"Oh Dorothy, she just came back to see her boyfriend. She's not my family. You're my daughter, you're the one who should be taking care of me. After all I've done for you, bringing you and your brother to this country, thousands of miles from my home, leaving everything and everybody who I hold dear! Working my fingers to the bone, for what? You only have one mother! You slut, you dared to abandon me and go gallivanting all over the world with some stew-pit man!"

"Mom, he's my husband! I have a family. I've always stayed in touch. We've brought you to Houston, Canada and even Indonesia to visit with us."

"You are my flesh and blood! That, Marion, is the truth, and you know it! I'm sick to death of you trying to fob me off and be rid of me. Well, my girl, you will never be rid of me. I'm your mother. I gave up everything for you. I've sacrificed my life and now you want to dump me in this hell hole?"

As I stare into her eyes, it is so clear; she is speaking with total conviction. I have no connection with my mother now—or ever! It's her story and nothing or nobody can change it. I sit back in the chair, letting what's happening between us sink in. I still feel desperate for at least some small positive acknowledgment from her...but the torpedoes are about to be launched!

Looking straight at me, her black eyes seeming suddenly to become two swirling pinwheels, she says, "*Marion, I am calling on god to curse you!* No good will ever come to you! I ask God to damn you to *hell* because of what you have done to me, your mother! *I curse you for all eternity!* Take me back to my room. I'm sick and tired of the sight of you!"

I feel the wind completely knocked out of me. Why? Why do these words of my mother shock me? I'm used to her telling me outlandish lies, carrying on about her miserable life, hitting me up for money, blaming me for leaving her and getting married. But cursing me because of what *I* have done to *her*?

She has never reached this level before. We're supposed to be Catholic for God's sake! For a Catholic, deliberately damning my soul is worse than pulling out a gun and shooting me! She wants God to damn my immortal soul?

I'm aware she has had a stroke and she is not in her right mind, but has she ever been? As I try to suck air back in to my lungs, tears well up in my eyes and all I want to do is scream, "*Shut up!*" at this old woman, sitting in a wheelchair beside a magnificent magnolia tree.

Mother or no mother, of all the things I've put up with over the years—how dare she curse me!

I sit stunned, not knowing if I'm going to laugh, cry, throw up, or explode! The voice inside me says, "Marion, calm down; she doesn't know what she's saying, she's had a stroke, she doesn't mean it."

Like hell, she always says what she means. This is what it has always been coming to—since the day I was born! My mother, the 'good' Catholic, who prays every night, goes to church every Sunday, who can be kind, joke and have fun with perfect strangers, but can sit in a wheelchair, look directly into my eyes, and deliberately demand God throw me in Hell because of what I have done to her? I can't cry, all I want to do is throw up!

The only person I can count on putting this in any perspective is my husband. He'll fall out of his chair laughing at my being cursed by Molly. Oh God, why can't I just laugh it off this time?

On my way out of town I stop off at Sacred Heart Church.

The candles are burning in front of the statue of Mary. I am numb.

Automatically, I light a candle and take out a piece of paper and pen from my purse.In front of the Blessed Mother I write on the paper.

I fold the paper up and bury it deep in a secret compartment of my wallet and deliberately leave the church without paying for the stupid candle.

A few days later, the nursing home calls me. I am summoned to a meeting with all the heads of the nursing home. The admissions officer, the head nurse, the floor nurse, a social worker from outside the facility, the director of the highly skilled nursing home and the office manager are all sitting around a large oval table in the conference room. I sit at the table and I think, "Well, Mom, you certainly have the power! This is definitely *hell*!"

I am told Molly has had a small stroke, affecting her right side. She has recovered remarkably well, nothing is wrong with her speech or her mind and with physical therapy she will, more than likely, fully recover. She is absolutely not eligible to stay any longer in Casa

Serena. I am told I need to make immediate arrangements to take Molly home with me.

What I want to say is, "Gee, sorry, no can do! Your patient, Molly Lewis, has put a curse on me so I'm off to Hell!"

The coward that I am, though, I say what my sister-in-law, a physical therapist, has told me to say; "I can't possibly take Molly home with me. Do you know she is incontinent?"

The head nurse looks at the floor nurse and asks, "Is that right?"

The floor nurse says, "I don't know, but I will find out."

The meeting with me is quickly adjourned. I am told this is an easy problem that will be resolved within a day or two. I must return to sign papers on Wednesday and I will definitely need to be prepared to take Molly out of Casa Serena on that day.

Chuck is in New Jersey working; Dorothy is not answering the door or the phone. I am totally numb as far as my mother is concerned. What will I do? What will happen? I have no idea.

As I walk up the path to the nursing home on Wednesday, the admissions officer, a large pretty woman who has been very condescending with me previously and adamant that I take Molly out of Casa Serena, comes running down the walkway to meet me. She is in a very agitated state. "Marion, quick, come with me. Don't let your mother see you!"

I follow behind her to a side door of the facility, wondering what on earth is going on. She has never addressed me as Marion before; she has always called me Mrs. Besmehn and referenced my mother as Mrs. Lewis. I am more than intrigued.

Now, Pat, my new best friend, who wears a small plastic name tag on her large bosom, complete with all kinds of professional letters behind her name, literally pushes me inside a staff office as she checks the hall both ways.

Inside the office, John, Molly's young social worker, who is actively investigating me for elder abuse, is standing by a table nervously shuffling papers. He acknowledges me, but quickly looks at Pat. John looks down at the table, as Pat looks directly at me and says, "We're going to meet with your mother across the building in the blue room. If you or she become unmanageable, we will stop the meeting immediately. You are not to upset your mother in any way. So I'm asking you to please not say a single word during the meeting, unless your mother gives you permission. Both John and I will tell you what we assess is best for your mother, based on her wishes. Agreed?"

"I'm not to say anything?"

"That's right. John and I think it best to let your mother do all the talking, and she will indicate what she feels is best for her."

All I can think is, "Oh great! I know my mother; she's going to talk and walk herself right out of here! Well, if she does, she's on her own, as I am going to be so out of here."

I hear the voice inside me say, "Right Marion, give Molly, long-lost Fred's number. She can call him to come pick her up!"

Pat looks at her watch and says, "We need to go. John, you go first. Molly usually walks the main corridors, so go the long way. I don't want Molly to see any of us, especially you, Marion, until we are situated in the blue room."

John gathers his papers and, looking sheepish, leaves the office. He is a clean-shaven young man in his early thirties. During the past week he had come to Molly's apartment and asked a thousand questions. Dorothy, who lives with my mother, has refused to see him. She is always 'out' when he comes to the apartment. She has taken to never answering Molly's telephone in case there are questions and she is told to come and collect Molly. Dorothy has told Casa Serena she is not a blood relation and cannot possibly be responsible for Molly. To say, "I understand," is an understatement.

"All right, Marion, follow me. Be prepared to run if we have to. I don't want your mother to even get a glimpse of you until we get to the blue room."

"I'm ready," is all I say. Pat checks each corridor before letting me continue to the blue room.

The blue room is a cozy sitting room which the patients are allowed to use with family members. It has a small round dining table with four chairs just opposite the door. The three of us claim chairs around the table, then Pat goes to the door to check if Molly is coming. I am sitting with Pat and John on either side. I can see straight out the door to the corridor.

Pat, at the door, says, "Okay, places people, here she comes. Now remember, Marion, smile and don't say a word."

Molly's profile appears in the doorway. Pat shrinks back from the door and takes her place at the table. Molly holds onto her walker, mostly with her left hand and arm. Her right side is still paralyzed but she is managing very well. She pushes the walker in a quarter turn. It makes an irritating scraping sound as it reluctantly turns on the corridor's shiny linoleum floor. The three of us sit in rapt attention as Molly completes the turn towards us and gives us the full effect of her entrance. Molly has had a permanent wave put in her hair. It is short, shiny, curly and dark as ever, with just a sprinkling of gray. Her dark eyes flash. She has on red lipstick, a little askew, and a white linen jacket I had brought her from home the day of the magnolia tree incident. Her figure is still slim and petite as always. After two weeks in Casa Serena, Molly is looking more and more herself.

There's a moment's pause; Molly focuses her eyes straight at me and says from the doorway, loud and clear, *"You bitch! You bitch!"*

Pat and John say in unison, "Now, Molly, none of that."

Mom completely ignores them as she advances toward me, pushing the walker with a vengeance. I automatically put my hand to my throat.

Pat tries to take charge and says in a soft voice, "Now, Molly, sit down and let's talk this over in a quiet..."

Molly doesn't hear a word. She stands over me and says, "You are the most pathetic excuse for a daughter the world as ever known.

You, my lady, will be paid back! God knows how you've treated me. He won't forget the curse I've put on you. How anyone can abandon her mother to this god-awful, disgusting place after all I have done for you is an outrage."

Whoa, I'm thinking, *Molly, these people can hear you!*

John rustles papers and tries to say, "We're here to discuss what's best for you."

Molly looks at him and says, "Shut up, this is none of your business; you're just a snot-nosed kid. I'm speaking to my good-for-nothing daughter, the daughter I have sacrificed my home, my mother, my father, my whole family—everything I hold dear. This bitch now leaves me here in this godforsaken place thousands and thousands of miles from where I belong. Well, Missy, I will not stand for this kind of treatment. Get me out of here, *now*, do you understand? Why God gave me such a selfish, stew-pit daughter I will never know."

Pat looks over to me and says, "She always talks to you this way?"

I smile (damn it, that was stupid), but Molly is on it. "Wipe that smile off your face, and you, you fat slob, don't you dare talk to my daughter; she knows nothing; you know nothing. I'm reporting all of you for being totally incompetent."

She takes a breath; she is exhausted. The stroke is taking its toll.

Pat and John take turns talking.

"Perhaps it could be arranged for you to live at your own place with help?

"Perhaps you would like to go into a residential home care?"

My mother has no interest in anything they are saying, she is concentrating on me. After a five minute rest Molly points her finger at my left hand. She blurts out, "My own daughter steals my mother's wedding ring from me! You little slut, you stole that ring from me. Give it back this instant! She points her finger in my eye and says, "*Now*, you slut!"

I look at John and with my eyes ask, "What should I do?"

Both his hands go up as if surrendering and he says, "Do what you want; say what you want."

I look straight at my mother and say, "No, this is my ring now. I asked you when I was married if I could have Grandma's wedding ring and you said you didn't care. I was married with this ring and I've worn it for twenty-seven years. So no, I will not give it back to you."

"Of course you won't; what can I expect from a worthless thief? Well, God knows what you've done. He knows how you have mistreated me and stolen everything I ever had. This, after I've worked my fingers to the bone. I sacrificed my life to bring you ungrateful children to this country, leaving the only home I've ever known. At least my mother and father loved me, not like you or your brother. Both of my children never loved me, my own daughter has never given a damn about me. You're the reason I'm stuck in this stew-pit place—penniless! Tell them how you stole all my insurance money—you won't get away with it, God will see to that. Damn you to Hell—and don't think I won't haunt you for the rest of your miserable life!"

Pat and John gather their papers and stand up. Pat says, above my mother's voice, "Okay, Molly, it's time for lunch. We have to take your daughter to the office to sign some papers."

I stand up. Molly abruptly turns from me, maneuvers her walker towards the door, and begins to shuffle out, still going on and on about how everything bad that's ever happened in her life is my fault. Her voice is more muffled and slurred now. Her exit is not nearly as strong as her entrance. She is tired and hungry.

My heart is beating fast, but I am definitely not as devastated as I was a week ago. In fact, I feel like clapping at my mother's brilliant performance.

Pat tells John and me to wait for a few minutes. She again checks the hall. "Good, Molly's gone around the corner. Quick, come with me." At the door, John says he has to get back to his office. I say good-bye and never see John again.

Pat has me follow her, but when we get close to the office, Pat's lookout comes and tells her that Molly's patrolling the hall in front of the office. Pat has me wait around the corner as she and the lookout watch for Molly. At the precise moment Molly turns the other way, I'm waved into the office quickly. Afraid Molly will come back and look through the office's glass partition, Pat tells me to get down on my hands and knees behind the desk. Molly does look.

After several minutes of me on my hands and knees waiting for Molly to stop looking in the window and leave the hall, the all-clear signal is given. I'm allowed to get up. I sign some papers and am told Molly can stay in Casa Serena until further notice. No one looks happy but me.

Has the stroke made my mother lose all control? Or has Molly orchestrated her own staying in Casa Serena?

In Casa Serena, Molly didn't have to cook or clean. She was surrounded with attention, social activities, dining facilities, physical therapy. I was told she regaled all the patients and staff with stories of her terrible, good-for-nothing daughter who had abandoned her, and the hard, hard life she had had in America. For the next four and a half years, Molly sailed on the good ship, Casa Serena.

1988

TOW TRUCKS

In 1988 Paul graduates from high school and my mother is in Casa Serena. Chuck asks me to move with him to Chicago.

One of the reasons I love Chuck is that he always consults the family when he's asked to move for work. We discuss what we feel is the best for all of us. We decide that, with Paul off to collage, I am free to go to Chicago.

So on my fiftieth birthday, I fly from San Francisco to Chicago to meet my husband and live on the 35th floor of the Presidential Towers in downtown Chicago.

As I pack the dishes to move to Chicago, my mother's voice tumbles around and around in my head. "Marion, you are as dull as dishwater and will never amount to a hill of beans, trust me!"

I've been married going on thirty years and have three grown sons. In the process I have washed, dried and packed a lot of dishes. I *am* a moving, boring dishwasher! What was it she said, I always wanted to be? A skivvy!

My mother has asked God to strike me down and throw me in Hell for being a dull as dishwater, stupid, skivvy daughter. She has a point!

Chicago is fabulous: tremendous energy, fantastic architecture, great art, but it doesn't last long. Something about a buy-out and we are on our way to Chuck's new job in Kingsport, Tennessee.

As menopause begins to catch up with me, I find myself, in the sixteenth move of my marriage, heading to rural Tennessee. I have to get my glasses and study the map. Now, where the hell am I going?

My marriage is as strong as ever; I have never seriously doubted my marriage. But I'd very much like a divorce from myself.

Then I read an ad in the Kingsport Times. It's October, and 20 miles away in Jonesborough, Tennessee, there is the National Storytelling Festival. "Come," the ad says, "and be transformed." Unfortunately, the first time I go to the storytelling festival, it is my car that is transformed.

I have since learned that Jonesborough, Tennessee, in autumn at the storytelling festival, is pure magic—if it weren't for the cars.

On the very first day I go to the Festival, I am running late. It is a Saturday, warm and sunny after a torrential rain the night before, and I have a ticket to hear Ed Stivender, and his story, *The Kingdom of Heaven is Like a Party,* at 1pm. But I can't find a parking space. I pass a huge wooden board splashed with white paint. "All Parking $10.00."

Okay, who do I pay? All I can see are parked cars. Up one street, down the other. I'm starting to panic. Finding a parking space is hell and I'm missing *Heaven and the Party.*

Suddenly, I see an old man standing in the middle of the street. I stop the car and ask, "Do you have a parking space for me?"

"Sure do, little lady, right over here." I look where he's pointing and sure enough, there's a space. The man walks over to the space and starts to direct me in parking my car. As I look over my shoulder and start to reverse, I see a large puddle, "must be left over from last night," crosses my mind as the parking attendant directs me into the space. It takes a nano second for my right rear wheel to plop straight down into the humongous hole, not a puddle. The parking attendant waves me forward. I shift the car into drive and step on the gas. The car makes a valiant try, and for its effort covers itself in mud. I am stuck, I can't go forward, I can't go back. No wonder nobody's parked here, but all I can think, "Do I still have to pay him the 10 dollars?"

After spinning my wheels for an eternity, the man comes over and says, "Gall darn, I'm sure sorry, little lady, I really shouldn't have done that—seein' as how I'm legally blind."

"You're not the parking attendant?"

"Hell no, I'm just waitin' on my daughter who's gone to listen to some fool story or other."

I can't tell you how dumb and stupid I feel at this moment. I have trapped myself in my car. The car I, myself, drove into a perfectly visible hole. My mother is so right, I am hopeless!

I carefully get out of my car into the sea of mud I've created and start walking down hill. At the bottom of the hill is a small grocery store. I ask to use their phone. Everyone is kind and sympathetic. I can't help feeling like such a stupid, over-the-hill, little old lady! They give me the number for the tow truck and I call. They have an emergency, but they will come as soon as they can. I go back up the hill and wait by my car. The car looks awful. It seems to have sunk even deeper into the hole. It doesn't look safe for me to crawl back in and hide.

People start coming back from being transported to *Heaven and the Party*. Everyone is in a great mood. I'm in my own private hell and I really don't want to talk to anybody. But no one, and I mean no one, passes me without trying to strike up a conversation.

"Is that your car? Oh honey, how awful."

"I saw that hole, knew that would happen."

"Oh no, you poor thing."

Cars leave, cars come back. Time for the evening show. I'm still waiting. People get out of their parked cars and start walking past me to the next story event. Again, nobody passes me without putting their two cents in.

"You still here? Boy, I'll bet you won't do that again!"

"I'm sure sorry, honey, but do your mommy and daddy know you're out with the car?"

"Lord, that's the funniest thing I ever did see!"

"I hate to say I told yaw so, but look there, Maude, didn't I always tell ya, she's the same as y'all—that little lady can't park neither!"

Finally, at 8pm I see the lights of a tow truck come up over the hill. The day has changed from a sunny, warm, autumn day, to an uncomfortable, chilly dusk, to a freezing pitch black night. I am numb with the cold. The tow truck gets me out of the hole as fast as I got myself in it. With my teeth chattering, I give my Visa card to the driver. He looks at me and says, "Ma'am, I'm not going to take your money. You had to wait all day because we had an emergency with a fool drunk driver and we only got one tow truck in these parts. I'm truly sorry. You get home to your husband, keep warm and drive safe now, ya hear?"

What can I say through my chattering teeth but "thank you"? I go home with the heater on full blast and a filthy dirty car.

My husband laughs at my story. He washes the car and takes me back to the festival the next day. After he parks the car, I am overwhelmed with the stories I hear and 'see' in my mind. I laugh; I cry. I am transformed.

After the parking incident I am suddenly so aware that my husband, Chuck, has been my biggest tow truck. I love him so much, and he has always been there for me.

I think about Mrs. Johnson, my professors in college, my good friends, Cindy (who I met when my boys were little), Rosemary, Sandy,

Marilyn and Joan from school—even strangers pulling my car out of the mud. They have all been my private tow trucks.

I am not my own person. I am a fifty year old woman who always tried to tell myself, "It's not the truth, it is not the truth!"

How pathetic! I am totally dependent on my husband, my friends, and other kind strangers to rescue me from all my stupidity and insecurity—oh God, my mother is right!

DAMN DUMPSTER

That's it! I am going to apply for admission to East Tennessee State University's Education Department's Master Degree program in Reading/Storytelling. Molly is not right! I won't believe her! Damn it, God give me strength!

I have the papers. I finally fill the papers out. I need to take them to the University as it's already too late to mail them. Chuck has to go on a business trip. I'm going to take him to the small airport in Kingsport and on the way home, I will drop the papers off at the University in Johnson City.

My mind keeps spinning, "Is my mother right, am I too stupid to do this? Am I too old? Will I be accepted? If I am, will I make a total fool of myself, as usual?"

My husband is out the door with his suitcase. I grab the papers and the garbage as I fly out the door and down the steps of our third floor apartment. He's at the car; I take the garbage to the dumpster. I lift the heavy lid of the huge dumpster and drop in the plastic garbage bag—along with my application to the Master's program. "Oh my God, no, no, please don't tell me!"

"Hurry up, Marion, it's getting late." He's putting his suitcase in the trunk.

I look down into the dumpster. The papers are lying face up on the very bottom of the empty dumpster, next to my one garbage sack. All thought stops as I drop my purse and stand on the curb to throw the lid of the dumpster wide open. Somehow I get one leg up and over the edge of the dumpster, and then the other; I truly have no idea how, but I do. I fall to the bottom, but miss falling directly on the papers. "Oh God, that's a good sign, right?" I pick myself and the papers up and then tuck them in the elastic waist band of my old lady pants. I want to throw up as I realize, "I have to get myself out of this hell hole! How did I get in?"

My whole life with my mother flashes before me:

YOU WERE NOT ONLY A STEW-PIT CHILD, YOU'RE A STEW-PIT OLD WOMAN! YOU'RE STILL NOT CAPABLE OF DOING ONE THING RIGHT!

Again her prediction is the truth! I have again trapped myself in a *hole*! What is wrong with me?

Enough is enough. *Shut the hell up, Mom!*

MARION, MARION!

Grandma, is that you?

MARION...

I hear my name again as I twist my hands and accidentally touch my wedding ring. Grandma's ring! Oh God!

I blindly jump up and grab the edge of the dumpster with both hands. "Dear Blessed Mary, Grandma, a boost?"

Somehow, one leg is up and over the edge of the dumpster. One more leg to go. "I beg you, please, please, you guys, get my other leg *(grunt, groan)* over this damn dumpster!"

Before I can adjust my balance, I tumble head-over-heels straight down. I pick myself up; miraculously, I'm on the *outside* of the damn dumpster and, even more miraculously, I'm standing on both legs. I take the papers from my waist band. The papers are intact! *I* am intact!

How did I do that? I can't even get out of a swimming pool without a ladder and a helping hand.

I have actually retrieved the papers with no damage and no help—*Ha!* Well, no visible help. Mom, put that in your pipe and smoke it!

My husband is sitting in the car with his mouth open. I walk over to the car and get in the driver's seat. "Did I just see you jump in the garbage dumpster and jump out?"

"Honey, do you remember the Appalachian folktale, 'Old Fire Dragaman?' In the story there is a magic ring that gets Jack out of the deep hole in the ground. We heard it told by Ray Hicks at the Storytelling Festival.

Well, maybe an old Welsh lady has a special ring with magical powers, too!"

MOLLY'S FINAL WORDS

I'm back for a visit in Salinas, from Kingsport, Tennessee. It's Christmas, and its been two and a half years since I've seen Molly, although I've kept in touch every week by telephone (fortified with a bourbon and soda). I get a report from the staff of how she's doing and even though Dorothy and the staff say my calls keep her going, she never recants her curse on me and reiterates it every time she gets me on the phone.

When I arrive at Casa Serena, she is sitting in a wheelchair by the window away from the main entrance. A nurse greets me and tells me Molly is just out of the beauty parlor, having had a permanent. The nurse laughs and says Molly is quite a character and has the whole staff of Casa Serena on their toes. Several times Molly has called an ombudsman. Casa Serena has had many extra unexpected visits to see if all the rules of an exemplary highly skilled nursing home are in effect. According to the nurse, mostly Molly's doing. The nurse tells me everyone in Casa Serena is aware of my mother and her power of words.

I walk over to where my mother is sitting and say, "Hi Mom, how's it going?" She looks up at me and says with no hesitation at all, "What the hell are you doing here? You needn't have bothered."

Her voice is strong, but she looks so frail in the wheelchair. I remember how mad she was at herself for not thinking of a wheelchair when she was vying for *Queen for a Day.* And it was from a wheelchair she first cursed me.

Same mother I've always known—only now she's Queen of Casa Serena, sitting in her wheelchair throne.

Oh God, I wish with all my heart I could tell her that I am back in college studying to be a storyteller. That she is my inspiration. Well, okay, that will never work.

Tears come to my eyes as she turns from me and wheels her chair away from the window and speaks directly to the nurse. The nurse smiles and winks at both of us as she walks away. I say out loud, "The boys and Chuck are coming to see you tomorrow."

Mom turns, looks up and asks, "Are you still married to that idiot?"

"Chuck? Yes, Mom, I'm still married."

"What he saw in a mouse like you I'll never know. You know his father stole a penny black stamp I put in Greg's (my oldest son) stamp book. I'll never forgive any of you for that betrayal!"

"Oh Mom, you are the master storyteller—where is this new story coming from?"

She goes on with utter conviction, "You're all living high on the hog from my Penny Black, a priceless stamp—for your information! While I'm stuck in this hell hole." She keeps going, hardly taking a breath, "Don't worry, you'll have your comeuppance very soon now. I've got your number, miss, you're not going to get away with any of it. You'll never outlive my curse. You just wait—God will pay you back for locking your own mother up, the mother who sacrificed everything, everything for you—do you understand? I'm asking God to curse you and throw you in hell for all eternity for what you've done to me, your own mother! Get out of my sight; I'm sick to death of you!"

My mother died peacefully in her sleep that night.

1992

TAKING MOLLY HOME

There is a funeral Mass for Molly. She is cremated. I am given her ashes.

I have finished all my course work at ETSU, and what I have to do next is my thesis. I need to collect and finish writing my Welsh stories and then video myself telling some of the stories.

In March of 1992, three months after Mom died, Chuck is transferred to London, England. Perfect: I'll go with Chuck and travel to Beaumaris with my mother's ashes to scatter on the family grave.

Chuck no sooner gets to London then he is transferred to Abu Dhabi, United Arab Emirates. I decide to take a flat in Beaumaris. I am excited to have time alone to write, and I will do the video in Beaumaris.

Walking with my mother's ashes, along the Beaumaris waterfront, then turning up the hill to the cemetery, my stomach starts churning the way it did when she was alive.

I arrive at the gate to the cemetery where I know Grandma and Grandpa are buried but I have no idea where. The sun is shining, but a cold wind has come up and is blowing hard, as a black cloud advances from across the water. As I stand by the gate I suddenly change my mind, I'm not going in! Maybe tomorrow.

The sun disappears behind the cloud. Suddenly, I feel a definite shove to my right shoulder, pushing me in the direction of the broken iron gate. I am completely alone; the only thing I can see and hear is the wind rustling the tall pine trees ringing the cemetery. With the hair on the back of my neck rising and my stomach churning, I try to breathe in the healing sea air. "Okay, okay," I hear myself say, "Don't push! I'll go, I'll go."

I squeeze through the broken gate and walk quickly along the gravel path, without looking right or left. The cemetery is overgrown with weeds. The headstones in the front of the cemetery are huge ancient monstrosities. Further along the path they give way to smaller tilted slabs so dirty it's impossible to read— especially if I'm unwilling to stop or turn my head! I walk to the very end of the path and am about to turn around, thinking that I'll never find them, when I see the name, "Gwyneth Paynter."

I stop and stare at the large clean headstone with her name so clear I couldn't possibly miss it. Written on the stone is "Seven and a half years old. Accidentally killed, 1946". It's my friend Gwyneth! Gwyneth's mother and father are buried next to her—and next to them are my grandmother and grandfather. I found them! I've walked straight to their graves!

I am the only living human being in the cemetery. I touch my grandmother's ring and know I am not alone.

Opening the box with my mother's ashes and dropping to my knees on Grandma and Grandpa's grave, with rain drops now plopping down on my head, I suddenly, unexplainably start sobbing. I can't stop. I cry so hard I throw up the hot cup of tea that I drank to fortify myself for this journey to the cemetery, right into the box of my mother's ashes!

Finally my meltdown is over and I sit back on my heels and blow my nose and wipe my eyes with a crumbled Kleenex. I look down at the tea, tears and huge rain drops sunk and sinking into the soggy sopping box of my mother's ashes. My mind flashes back to the explosion of the beans on the ceiling in Lewis' Coffee Shop. The box of ashes has no color or shape; it's just a total, sodden mess. Nothing like the beautiful ceiling, but I make the connection and now I can't stop laughing. "Oh God, Mary, Gwyneth, Grandma,

Grandpa, give me strength! And Mom, do you think maybe now, you'll leave me in peace?"

Is it over? This is easier than I thought.

WISHFUL THINKING

I have an aunt and a cousin still living in Beaumaris. Auntie Mabel had married my mother's youngest brother, Harold. They had one child, Sylvia, who was born with one leg shorter than the other and a lump between her shoulders that grew to the size of a soccer ball. Uncle Harold had died in the 1970s.

Now, 1993, Sylvia, Mabel's only child, is running a pet owner's store. She and her mother are still living above the shop that Uncle Harold and Auntie Mabel had bought in 1938. The building they bought was once part of the Old Bull's Head Inn, nowadays a very posh hotel, built in the fifteenth century with the thirteenth century castle just up the street.

My Auntie Mabel is getting on in years, and both mother and daughter are adamant: relative or not, I am *not* to go around telling stories of my Grandmother and Grandfather Lewis in Beaumaris. Sylvia tells me she is in business and can't be linked with a grandfather who took to drink after the First World War. Auntie Mabel said it is no use bringing up the past as it is nobody's business. Both seemed very suspicious of what I am trying to do.

I rent a video camera and set it up to record my stories in secret. I was feeling good about the work I'd done, until I sent the tapes back to my son, John, to be edited. He called me on the phone to tell me the tapes were blank! "You have to press the record button Mom, plus it's a different system in Britain!"

I am becoming more and more overwhelmed with what I want to do and what I can not get done in this medieval place. Molly's words keep knocking constantly against my brain. I am not only as dumb and as dull as dishwater, but I am a silly, slow, stupid, simpering stooge, who cannot do one thing right if my life depends on it. I can clearly hear her say, "The only thing you're good at, me lady, is being a skivvy!"

One night, I am invited to have dinner at Auntie Mabel and Sylvia's. It is late November; in fact, at home it's around Thanksgiving. I am so grateful that they have invited me. It is, of course, a freezing, blustery, miserable Beaumaris night. I arrive in the dark a little before five o'clock. The shop is still open and Sylvia says that Auntie Mabel is waiting for me and to go straight up the narrow steps to the living quarters. I have never before been invited to dinner or been up the stairs and into their living space.

I start up the ancient, narrow, winding stairs to find myself on a landing with two doors, one on the left, one on the right, with the winding stairs continuing up. The almost closed door to the left seems to float in space. It is above the landing with no real step up, just a large gap. I lean over and look up and in, behind the almost shut door, a toilet and sink. An indoor bathroom! Obviously, a fairly recent convenience that looks positively dangerous! How on earth do they manage? The tightly shut door to the right must be the sitting room. It has a black, old-fashioned telephone on a small table, just outside the door.

I knock and hear a cat meow. I gingerly turn the doorknob and open the door. Auntie Mabel sits in a chair facing the door, wrapped in a soft, fawn-colored cashmere blanket with a large, hard to distinguish, ginger cat in her lap. She looks up and waves me in. The sitting room is tiny but cozy. The electric fire is on. Red velvet panels with white lace curtains hang down two windows that look out onto Castle Street. The window panes are being battered with rain and wind.

Auntie Mabel says to shut the door tightly, as that is how they try to keep the heat in. She tells me to sit down and pick up the gin and tonic she has waiting for me on the side table. I sink into the small settee and take a couple of swallows of the bitter drink. I begin to thaw out as I slip out of my heavy parka and notice that Auntie Mabel has almost finished her gin and tonic. She says, "It's nineteen years ago to the day Harold died, right where you're sitting."

"Oh my gosh, really?" I jump up, but I realize I have to sit back down, as now I really need another swallow of my gin and tonic.

As Auntie Mabel pours more gin and no tonic into her glass, she leans back in her chair and says, "My parents both died when I was two years old, my father from the effects of World War I and my mother from the Spanish flu outbreak. I don't remember either one of them. I remember my brother John, but he was so much older; I don't remember him being around very much. My two sisters were also older, and I was kept away from them, too. Betty was born with brittle bones. She only had to turn over in bed to break a bone. My other sister, Violet, is the sister I thought of as my mum, even though I didn't see her very much. Sometimes she would come to see me on a weekend and she always brought me a little gift. A hair ribbon or a piece of soft candy."

Auntie Mabel pours more gin into her glass and I am both fascinated and shocked that she is willing to tell me all this.

"When my Mum and Dad died, my father's two older sisters took me in. They thought a two-year-old would be easier to cope with than my sisters and brother. I'm afraid I wasn't. As I grew up, I only wanted to be with Violet. But my aunts said I had to stay with them and behave myself. I ran away more than once. Violet always brought me back and said things would be better when I was grown-up and I could live with her forever."

Mabel has a far away look in her eyes. I'm not sure she's talking to me as she says in a whisper, "I still can't believe Violet went away without me." She takes a sip of her drink and looks at me. "Your mother left for America a couple of years after I was married. John, my brother, took Betty and Violet to Australia." She laughs as she takes another sip, "I've never said this out loud and I would never tell Sylvia—but the truth is, I have never gotten over Violet leaving me."

She puts the cat on the floor and stands up. She goes over to a small dark sideboard and rummages in a bottom drawer. She comes away holding a photograph. She goes over to her chair and sits down, but holds the photograph out to me. I get up and take the picture, then sit back down to have another quick drink of my gin and tonic. I have never seen this photo before. Auntie Mabel says it's a picture of her wedding to Uncle

Harold in 1935. The bride and groom sit on a bench on the church grounds surrounded by family.

I recognize my grandmother: She stands rigid. She is wearing her good wool coat, a sepia felt hat with a feather, a black velvet choker, an orchid corsage on her lapel, and very shiny shoes. She clasps her hands in front of her. Her mouth is pulled into a thin, rigid line. Her eyes stare into the camera with the same look I remember when Grandma and Grandpa huddled around the wireless, listening to news of the war. My Grandma looks sick with worry. The groom, Molly's youngest brother, Harold, sits next to his bride looking petrified. His hair is plastered down and his ears stick out. His face is beyond serious, with frown lines popping out on his small boyish face. He is a child in grown-up men's clothes!

The bride, my Auntie Mabel, is sitting next to her unhappy husband. She wears a white dress with veil and looks so sweet, pretty, and nowhere near old enough to be married. The bride and groom in the photograph look like children playing wedding dress up!

Mabel tells me it is her sister, Betty, standing next to her in the picture. Betty's face is pinched and there are dark circles under her eyes. Mabel says, "Betty was in constant pain and was in and out of hospital all her life. That's my brother, John, standing behind Harold." He looks big, strong, annoyed.

Mabel tells me the person standing a little apart on Mabel's right is her beloved sister, Violet. She looks so sad, as if she is attending a funeral. Neither of the sisters look dressed for a wedding, have shiny shoes, or are wearing hats. There is another woman standing next to John, I assume it is John's wife. But it is not. It is a friend of my mother's. (Years later when Aunty Mabel allowed me to have the picture copied and I showed it to my cousin, Shirley, she told me it is Sissy Williams, who was invited at the last minute by my mother, much to Grandma's annoyance.)

There are two bridesmaids in the picture, standing up behind Harold and Mabel. I don't need to be told who they are. One is a much younger friend of my mother's. I've met her; she still lives next door to Mabel and Sylvia. She is wearing lace and a stylish, large floppy hat and looks delighted to be in the wedding. The other bridesmaid is Molly, my mother. She is wearing a lovely lace dress and an absolutely gorgeous picture hat. She is smiling and looks radiant. Shirley, my cousin, who is four years old in 1935, is kneeling in the front row next to a young boy; Mabel says she has no idea who he is. (Shirley doesn't remember either. We think it might be Grandma's grandson, Frank, visiting his Grandmother and Grandfather. Frank's father, Uncle Johnny, left Beaumaris to marry Laura.)

Mabel goes on, "As I got older, my aunts said I had to go to nursing school. I was young, I was foolish, and I did not want to go to nursing school. That's when I met Molly, your mother, at a dance in Llandudno. Molly was the same age as my sister Violet. Molly invited me to come to Beaumaris. I went and Molly introduced me to Harold. He was a sweet young man. We were both so young and innocent. I met your grandmother; she was kind, but to tell you the truth, I never got on with her.

"Molly was my champion. She was so concerned with my aunts forcing me to go to nursing school; she said that was not fair. Molly said to come and stay in Beaumaris with her. She had just taken a small cottage across the street from the Catholic Church. That was when your grandmother had set your mother up with a little notions shop on Church Street. Molly said I could work in the notions shop and stay with her and earn my keep. I wouldn't have to go back to school—or my aunts.

"Molly told me she thought I would really be good for Harold. She said the whole family was so worried that he was immature and didn't know what to do with his life. Molly said he just needed a good hard working woman like me, who could take care of him. I began to think I would be good for Harold: I would be a good wife, and I would work hard.

"My aunts found out I was living and working in Beaumaris with Molly Lewis. They sent a letter to your grandmother telling her that I was to come home immediately. I was underage and I had an obligation to become a nurse and take care of them in their old age, as they had taken care of me. Your mother saved me. She told your grandmother that my aunts were unreasonable and I didn't want to become a nurse; besides, Harold and I were getting married and I was willing to become a Catholic!

"Molly said it was the perfect answer for both Harold and me. I would at last have a family of my own and I would have no more obligation to my aunts. Molly said Harold would, at last, have someone his own age that was sensible and had a good head on her shoulders. Molly said Harold and I were the perfect couple. I thought we were, too. We were married on my twenty-first birthday. Harold and I were both born the same year. I tried the best I could and I think we would have had a chance, if it hadn't been for Lena O'Brien."

Lena O'Brien? I look up at Auntie Mabel: Good God in Heaven! I take a huge gulp of my gin and tonic as I stare back at the photograph. My mother didn't? Oh, God! Of course, she did!

Mabel had closed her eyes after putting down her empty glass. She whispered, "I still can't get over Violet leaving me and never coming back to Wales."

I can hear Sylvia in the kitchen putting the dinner on the table. She must have come up the back stairs. I didn't know there were back stairs in such small quarters, but if Sylvia was in the kitchen, there had to be a back stairs. Back stairs that had been planned and constructed, just like the added convenience, and just as Mabel becoming a Catholic and marrying Harold, had to be planned and carried out by someone who knew perfectly well what they were doing. Looking at the picture, it is so obvious it was not the bride or groom!

I give the photo back to Mabel and she says as an afterthought, "All the time we were married I knew Harold went to Manchester to see Lena, every chance he got. She was the only woman he ever loved. You know, she never married."

My poor Auntie Mabel didn't want to be a nurse, but she desperately wanted a family.

I could see my Auntie Mabel had tears in her eyes. She didn't have to tell me what happened after the marriage, as everyone in the family and all of Beaumaris knew.

After Sylvia was born, Uncle Harold never had a civil word to say to Mabel. But because Sylvia was disabled, because they were married in the Catholic Church, because they lived in a small medieval town in North Wales, there was no hope of a second chance for either one of them.

My mother was aware of all that was going on in Beaumaris, from letters. When she got a letter from Beaumaris, she always announced it was such a shame Harold had married Mabel and it certainly was not the fault of the Lewis family that caused Sylvia's disability. I came to understand Mom meant "genes" when she said, "fault," whether she knew it or not. Mom said she always knew Mabel wasn't really "our kind." After seeing the photograph, I now understand what "our kind" means: those who dress up, wear hats and shine their shoes!

Sylvia opened the door to the tiny dining room and asked us to come to the table. We sat down, but Auntie Mabel immediately excused herself, saying she was afraid she was not feeling well. She left the table and Sylvia and I were alone. Sylvia said she hoped the meat was not too well done for me. It was, but I said it was very good of her to have me over on a work day. I think that was about all we talked about. Oh yes, we did talk about the cats and Sylvia's two pet sea gulls, Harriet and Horace, who came to the kitchen window sill every evening to be fed. I wanted to help with the dishes, but Sylvia said absolutely not. I was to get back to my flat as quickly as I could, before the rain came again, and it was already very unseemly for me to be seen alone on the street this time of night.

Walking back to the flat I was sick to my stomach, realizing what my mother had done.

Lena O'Brien was my mother's best friend! Mom talked about her all the time. Lena and her mother lived in Manchester, but they came to Beaumaris often.

Lena was a pretty, plump Irish girl, the same age as my mother, six years older than Harold. I'd seen her picture many times.

When Mom had a cigarette and was in the right mood, I often remember her saying, "Nobody could make Harold laugh like Lena."

My mother must have 'found' Mabel to marry Harold because she didn't want her brother to get mixed up with her best friend. Lena and Harold liked each other and had too much fun together. Of course, her excuse was that Lena was too old for Harold. Knowing my mother, it is as plain as the nose on my face: Molly was jealous! After all, two years later, in 1937, Molly herself married a man thirty years older than she was.

Molly and Beaumaris are both a horrible nightmare, and I can't wake up! Next day I stop by the shop to thank Auntie Mabel and Sylvia for having me to dinner. Sylvia says she'd tell her mother, as her mother is resting and not seeing any visitors today. She also says it was not very wise of me to let her mother and myself drink so much. I don't tell Sylvia that I only had the one gin and tonic. Sylvia was right, though: digging up the past and reliving how Molly operated is more than enough reason for all of us to stay away from gin!

They are both relieved when I announce I am leaving early. I have to get out of Beaumaris! The longer I stay, the more paranoid I am becoming. I imagine Molly's power swirling in and around me. I am convinced my mother never gives up. She always gets her way—alive or dead!

I am on a plane home within the week— the only problem being that I do not *have* a home. Chuck is still overseas, and our plan has been to save all the money we can, so that after our youngest son and I graduate, we can buy a house. Then Chuck and I will have a home to call our own.

Before I leave Beaumaris, I call my friend Joan, who now lives in Carmel, California. Chuck and I have always loved the Monterey Peninsula. It's twenty miles from Salinas, on the sea, and the weather is a lot warmer than North Wales.

Joan comes to my rescue. She finds a room for me over her friends garage and helps me figure out all the resources I need, to complete the video.

1994

CARMEL

Living over a garage in Carmel, California, I have been approved to graduate with my master's degree in storytelling at the end of May. It is almost the end of April and I have finished writing the story of *Molly and Bill,* when the nightmare takes over.

Mom and I are on a school bus. It is driving over very bumpy ground. Molly is sitting alone, directly in front of me. She turns around, wags her index finger in front of my nose, looks me in the eye and says, "MARION, YOU KNOW PERFECTLY WELL, YOU ARE GOING TO HELL!"

The school bus stops dead in its tracks. I am thrown violently forward and am suddenly falling out of control, down a black hole full of stinging grit and debris. I can hear Molly's voice, booming through a powerful sound system, *"GOING TO HELL, GOING TO HELL."*

Every morning I bolt awake, sick to my stomach and covered in sweat. I struggle to my feet and throw cold water on my face and every morning I look into the mirror. "Oh, God, give me strength!"

I'm feeling more and more sick to my stomach and weak. Am I doing the wrong thing, writing about her? Is she paying me back for having the audacity to write what I believe is the truth? *Is* it the truth—or my imagination?

Then the spot appears.

One day it is just there, on the back of my right leg. Black, purple, asymmetrical, the size of an eraser at the end of a pencil. I know it is not good, but I promise myself; no matter what, I will graduate. I have to do one thing right, come hell or high water.

I have made a very special friend in Kingsport. She is the one who insisted I sign up for the graduate program at ETSU. She and her husband have cried and laughed at my stories. When Chuck had to leave Kingsport before I finished my course work, Deanna and Jim insisted I stay the summer with them before I left for Wales.

Chuck is transferred back to Houston, and both of us meet at Deanna and Jim's house. I cross the stage of ETSU to pick up my diploma, praying the bandaid is holding the blood from trickling down my leg.

Two days after I graduate, Chuck and I fly back to Houston, his new assignment, and I am promptly diagnosed with stage four melanoma.

HOUSTON

All I can think is, "This is Molly's doing!" I have been referred to M.D. Anderson Hospital in Houston. When we call, they can't take me for three weeks. We call a good friend of mine who I had met the last time we were in Houston with our boys. Liz has four boys and, when I knew her, she was getting her doctorate in nursing. She refers us to a small, innovative cancer clinic. It is Friday, we call and get an appointment right away. Surgery is then arranged for the following Monday.

Chuck takes me out for a drink. We sit at the bar in a restaurant called *Houston's*, in Houston, Texas. I proceed to cry into my bourbon and soda, "Please don't remarry too soon." I finger the long rope of real pearls I am wearing, a wonderful surprise gift from Chuck years ago.

When our boys were young and we were living in Grande Prairie, Alberta, Canada, I had played Yenta, the matchmaker, in the community production of *Fiddler on the Roof*. Years later, when we were in Hong Kong, Chuck bought me a long rope of real pearls in remembrance of my role in *Fiddler on the Roof*.

"I love you, I love our boys! I just don't have the strength to fight my mother anymore; ever since Beaumaris I feel I really am in her clutches—and she's bound and determined to do me in!"

Suddenly, holding up my pearls I blurt out, "Chuck Besmehn, if you ever dare give these pearls to another woman, I swear I'll haunt the two of you!"

Chuck chokes on his drink. I realize I have just said the words from *Fiddler on the Roof*! We look at each other and almost fall off our bar stools laughing. Chuck grabs hold of my hand, squeezes it, looks straight into my eyes and says, "Honey, I know what you've been through with your mother—and now this; but believe me, she has nothing to do with it. Don't go there! One of the things I love about you is that you've always known from the start that your mother had it totally wrong. You know perfectly well she really was off her rocker! Don't you dare start going to the dark side and believing all her lies." Now his eyes twinkle. "Besides," he continues, "do you know what a pain it would be for me to have to buy a different necklace for another woman?"

Holding on to my husband's hand for strength, I come up out of the thick black Molly hole I've let myself sink into. We have a plan.

Whatever the outcome, he'll be with me all the way—and in the long run, if I do pop off, and if he does pick another wife, and he does give her my pearls, God help me, I love him so much, I'll try not to be too burnt up about it! Oh, God, I am my mother's daughter!

Monday, both the surgery and the chemotherapy put through my leg go well. After nine days I am released from the hospital.

Chuck gives up an assignment in South America and tells the company he wants to stay in Houston to be close to my doctors, to be sure I am out of the woods.

SALVATION ARMY

We are in Houston, six years before Chuck will be able to retire. I belong to the Houston Storytellers Guild, and with the help of my friend Liz, I get a volunteer job, telling stories at the Salvation Army's women and children's shelter.

The facility the Salvation Army owns is an old motel in downtown Houston. There is no room available for me to tell stories to the children at the shelter, so I have the children sit on the floor of the old lobby. I am amazed at how much the children pay attention and love to hear old-fashioned fairy tales. We have very little room to spread out, but I tell a story to the kids. The children repeat the story back to me and I assign volunteers to play the characters in the story. It is so good to see the children think, laugh and learn using their imaginations. I am convinced that children who are able to concentrate on a story, through listening and then acting out the story, with no audience but each other—are teaching themselves a lot about life and who they are. In my mind, the more fun they have, the more they learn.

When I was at East Tennessee State University, I learned folktales of the

Appalachian, all-American hero, Jack. The children in the shelter love Jack. In many ways, Jack is very much like these children. He is poor, only sometimes has a mother or father, and usually has two brothers, Will and Tom. He gets into great difficulties, but he is always kind, uses his wits, is willing to share, and always gives a helping hand. The children laugh and marvel at how Jack consistently manages to land on his feet. Jack is not a superhero in the modern sense, but the children love him. He is a good role model. I have long imagined a girl, maybe a Jackie, who saves the day as Jack does.

At the Houston Storytellers Guild, I write a story of a modern day Jackie. My Jackie is a middle-aged woman, exhausted with the Christmas pressures of her mother, who insists she crank out hundreds of Christmas letters with an exposé of the whole year of family woes —her mother-in-law, who comes to Jackie's house, turns her kitchen upside-down and bakes dozens and dozens of Christmas fruit cakes as heavy as bar bells.

The Guild hires me to tell the story to a Ladies Christmas Lunch, in a large Protestant Church. It does not go well. Houston ladies are not amused with my hero, Jackie, saving the day by buying two tickets for her and her husband to fly to Paris and escape, for once, the whole commercial hoop-la of Christmas. It doesn't seem to help, at the end of the story, to have the middle-age couple, hand-in-hand, contemplating the beautiful rose window in Notre Dame Cathedral, in Paris.

Telling my Beaumaris stories to the women at the shelter is also useless. I try to make them laugh with stories of my grandmother, and grandfather and Wales. Who knows where Wales is? I try a simple story of Molly finding a way to circumvent one of her mother's rules.

After the Molly story, one of the women comes up to me and tells me that the main reason she is in the shelter is because her mother threw her out, her and her three-year-old little girl. She says she wants to write a letter to her mother. With tears in her eyes, this young woman says, "I'd really like to tell that old bat what I think! She never listens. She thinks she knows everything."

I say, "Okay, I understand. Why don't you take some time and write what you want to say to your mother. If you're here next week and you want me to, I'll listen to it. I don't have any answers, but I have lots of experience with a crazy mother."

The next week, I bring spiral notebooks and ballpoint pens for everyone in the class. The same young girl is back. I can tell that she is bursting to talk. I let her. She tells the class how her boyfriend, not the father of her child, beat her up. When she took her little girl home to her mother, her mother said she was through rescuing her and her "bastard child." That's why she is in the shelter. She calls it "the dump."

I ask her if she has written the letter to her mother? She says, "No, but I've been thinking about it all week."

I hand her a notebook and pen. "Okay, write the letter to your mom." I hand each of the women a notebook and pen. "The rest of you, write to whoever or whatever you want; it is your book to keep and whatever you write is your own private business. If you want to share, we'll listen. Nobody cares about spelling or grammar, so say whatever you want. You can always tear it up when you're finished. If you don't want to write, then you can draw a picture or make a grocery list."

After a while, I ask the young woman, "Do you want to read the letter to your mom?" She does, and everyone is interested in what she wrote. I tell the class that whatever she reads to us is for the class alone. Nothing that is read or discussed in class must go outside the class.

Everyone embraces the mad, sad, bad of what is read out loud. Everyone has an opinion.

I try to ask the reader if it is all right to discuss her work? But the class is already in a heated discussion before I finish asking the question.

After that, I have them write every week. Lots of times, the women bring the notebook they had gotten the week before and want to read what they had written during the week. There is a high turnover, and I certainly don't always see the same women the second or third week. Not one woman refuses a notebook and pen, though. Every week I have a full class.

Some days, amazing things are read. It can be heartbreaking, maddening, soul-searching, crazy. From what they write I come to a better understanding of what these women face everyday: physical violence, verbal abuse, numbing poverty—things much worse than I have had to put up with.

As a child I knew sexual abuse from a father and verbal abuse from a mother. I am qualified, as is everyone else in the class, to listen to writings of women trying to understand who they are, and the truth of what has happened and is happening to them.

One thing is very evident: most of us have known betrayal from the people we love.

God give us all strength.

In 2000, Chuck retires, and we move to Carmel, California.

1940 — 2005

BILLY, MY BROTHER

The only family member I haven't said much about is my brother, Billy, seventeen months younger than me.

"Billy" is what Grandpa, Grandma, Mom and I always called him. He was "Bill" to his wife and friends. Billy left my life and Mom's when he was fifteen and in truth before that. His only contact with us was when he needed money. I had no contact with him for years. I called him when Mom had the stroke. He would not come to see her. I called several times and when she died, he would not come to the funeral; but my calls put us back in touch.

He had been drinking and smoking since he was fifteen. His wife divorced him because of his drinking, and he got cancer from his smoking.

Not long after Mom died, he became critically ill. I saw him several times before he died. Even though it was too late to talk, I saw how much he loved his ex-wife and daughter, who were both by his side. I even saw in his eyes his love for me.

Billy's and my story has at least that much of a happy ending.

2010

THE QUEEN MARY

I've been writing steadily for the last five days. I need to wrap this up. I feel I've done what I needed to do. Yet the truth is that I'm not feeling anywhere near what I imagined I'd feel. Through the years since Mom's death, I had convinced myself that if I got it all out, if I just told my whole truth, it would miraculously make everything all right between us and then, when the time came, both of us could rest in peace. How stupid can I be? She died cursing me. End of story!

I get up from the chair I've been sitting in all morning and head back to our cabin. I've got to get rid of this computer. I have written way too much. I'm fed up with myself, the computer and Molly.

I walk back into the Commodore Bar, this time by myself. No laptop, no Chuck, and thanks be to God, no voice of Molly in my head!

I have a date in three hours to have a drink with Chuck and supposedly celebrate my getting my story finished. I hope I'm sober by the time he gets here!

I order a glass of wine at the bar and turn myself around to look out the floor-to-ceiling windows. I watch as the Queen glides seamlessly through the endless sea. Not as endless as when we started this journey. I'm realizing that this ship is only twelve hours away from the coast of England! I will not be on the water on the QM2 tomorrow afternoon—or likely ever again.

For God's sake, what's my problem? Why is my mother and her curse such a big deal? What would my grandmother say? "Why can't ya let sleeping dogs lie?" Actually no, she'd not say that. But Grandpa might.

Grandma would say, "Good God in heaven, that's not how Molly was brought up. I know she is a terrible handful, but Marion, she's your mother, she's my daughter! You have to know she didn't mean, didn't understand, what she was saying! For God's sake, Marion, put it right!"

"Grandma! It's way too late. How the bloody hell can I put it right? Molly was Molly. She couldn't stand the sight of me. She said what she said and then she died! I know how much you loved her; I know how much you prayed for her. Grandma, I am so sorry! I was my mother's greatest disappointment. Now it looks like I will be yours, too!"

I turn to the bar and take the napkin under my wine glass and dab my eyes. The bartender is looking at me, but trying not to. His name is Ivan, and he brings me my tea every morning. He knows I'm writing about my long dead mother. No doubt he thinks, "Poor old lady, she misses her mother and the good old days!"

I pick up my wine glass and move to a small table in the corner that's just been vacated. I sit down and fight back the tears trying to fill my eyes. I take my wallet from my purse. I find the piece of paper. I've been too stew-pit to dump after only 25 years. Of course, I haven't been too good at dumping my mother, either! I open the folded paper as I slip my reading glasses from my forehead and read out loud what I wrote in Sacred Heart Church in front of the Blessed Mother, so very long ago: *"Mother of God, my own mother has just cursed me! What in God's name do I do now?"*

Suddenly, I'm choking. My mother's voice is back, loud and clear!

YOU ARE A STEW-PIT, SKIVVY, SLUT! NO GUMPTION, THAT'S YOUR PROBLEM! NO GUMPTION, NO GUMPTION!

Ivan comes over to my table and asks if I am okay, and would I like another glass of wine?

Cough, cough, stutter, I shake my head and say, much too loudly, "I need something stronger!"

Without warning I look up at the ceiling and scream at the top of my lungs, *"It's hopeless. I give up. You win!"*

The other waiter behind the bar comes running over as Ivan says, "Oh my goodness, Mrs. B, are you all right? I bring you a whiskey quick!"

He snatches my empty wine glass, turns and runs to the bar as the other bartender reaches my side and asks what's going on. "Is that guy bothering you, Mrs?"

Oh my God, I can't believe I did that! I'm mortified. "No, no, I'm sorry, please forgive me. Silly, stupid me, I just forgot to take my pills. Ivan is getting me a drink I'll be fine. So sorry for the disturbance; it won't happen again."

I see the few people scattered around the room turning to look at me. I hear a man say, "Oh, it's just that crazy old lady who's always here. She finally popped her cork!" The three other people are looking my way and laughing.

Great, I've managed to make myself a public spectacle, and I just lied to the bartender! Pills? What pills? Oh, my God! *I am my mother!*

I slump back in my chair and drop the paper, which I've somehow wadded into a small ball, on the table. My reading glasses fall off my head next to it. Dear God, what a mess! Well, Mom, there is absolutely nothing I can do before I die to make any difference to the story of you and me. You are right, have always been right. I am the biggest, silliest sluttiest, stupid skivvy that the world has ever known! Your words! And guess what? I am in Hell! Finally facing the reality that I really am what you always said I was: useless.

Ivan is back with a highball glass half full of straight whiskey, no ice. I think to myself, "Great, whiskey *is* the only answer I have for dealing with you, Mom!"

"Thanks, Ivan. Please forgive me for the outburst."

"No worries, Mrs. B. You have trouble with Mr. B?"

Oh geez, Chuck—I forgot! "No, no. I'm just under a lot of pressure writing my memoirs. You know Ivan, telling the truth is a real bitch!" I take a tiny sip of the whiskey, It burns my throat as I swallow. Ivan smiles and nods his head. He is the perfect bartender, the perfect listener. "Ivan, if you see my husband, would you tell him I've jumped overboard! According to my mother, I would never have the gumption to do that. Don't worry; she's right. I don't and I won't."

I take another sip of the whiskey. "You know, Ivan, once my Grandma drank whiskey to give her the gumption to tell Grandpa what he had to do to get out of the mess he was in. So I have to drink this whiskey to get up the gumption to tell my husband that I cannot do what he was so sure I could do! My grandmother and Chuck really believed I could pull off telling the story of Molly and me and come up with a satisfactory ending for all concerned. But, obviously, there is no way on God's green earth that I can do it." I take another sip of the whiskey. "Ivan, do you think whiskey will give me the gumption to reconcile myself with being a complete idiot?"

Ivan is standing in front of me. I look straight up into his face and know that he has no idea what I am talking about. But I can see in his eyes his concern for me. Perhaps he, too, has a crazy mother back in Poland? Amazingly, I can elicit a connection from a bartender doing his job but have never, ever had the ability to connect with the woman who gave birth to me!

"Ivan, did you know that it is hell to wallow in self-pity?"

"Mrs. B, I bring mug of black coffee, okay?"

"Whatever, just don't tell Mr. B. I'm here—comprendre?"

Ivan returns to the bar, leaving me to wallow in Hell, alone. But hang on. If I know my mother, any second she'll be back in my head, having a field day! *Please, just let me close my eyes for a few minutes of silence...*

What on earth? Lifting my head off the table I'm hearing a boisterous commotion of people coming into the bar. What a racket! I've got to get out of here. Can I walk? Boy, do I feel shaky. There is an empty glass and a cup of stone-cold coffee in front of me. I have no recollection of Ivan bringing me the coffee.

How long have I been sitting here? I have got to move. I have no idea what time it is. I need to find Chuck.

Gathering my glasses, purse, I notice the worthless wad of paper rolling off the table and on to the floor. Reaching down to retrieve it, I clunk my head on the table. Ouch!

Looking up I see reflecting in the window a wheelchair coming in the lounge. Wait a minute! That's—not, no, it can't be!—Mom? Molly! Oh my God, I am sailing right into hell! *You? My mother? On the Queen Mary?*

Please no, no—I'm losing it! This is not good! Jumping overboard is definitely preferable. I've spent way too much time on that damn computer. Okay, as God is my witness, I am actually seeing my mother being wheeled to a table right in front of me!

Oh my God, this is *not* happening! Whoever, whatever this, this...mirage...is, she's, she's...looking fabulous! She's wearing a gorgeous gold lame evening gown! Oh, my God, that dress is the same dress my mother wore when she went to that bingo dance with Fred! I love that dress!

She's with a group of people. Oh, no, no, this is insane! I know those people! They're all *dead!* Jack Bailey. Auntie Mabel. Uncle Harold. Lena O'Brien and Fred. Oh God, I really do see them! Am I dead? I am in hell, right?

They're standing right in front of me! Wait, wait...I can hear Molly's voice but it's *not* in my head; it's coming from where she's sitting in that bloody wheelchair! Oh my God, she's telling her famous Megan Lloyd George sob story! Everyone around the table is beside themselves, hanging on her every word. They all have handkerchiefs. Well, maybe not Fred, but he is listening intently and nodding his head.

This is just not possible—is it? Jack Bailey is reaching over to a red velvet box beside him and pulling out...oh, my gosh, a drop-dead, glorious, fabulous, double-diamond tiara!

Dear Mother of God, my mother is looking over here. She sees me. Our eyes are meeting! Oh, good grief—what's happening?

Molly's eyes are looking straight at me. She knows me. I feel the electricity between us.

Oh God, now what's happening? I'm feeling all the pain, all the anger, all the nausea, my mother has caused me. It's...it's all coming out, it's leaving me! I feel and see it leaving. I can actually see and feel it sliding out of my head and my heart! Oh my God, there it is...a huge pool of beautiful colored chaos on the floor right in front of me! I see the colors—and I'm color blind! Reds, greens, yellow, orange, all swirling, writhing, disappearing!

Blessed Mother, yes, yes, I can live and die with this.

Everyone is clapping as Jack crowns my mother with the diamond tiara and proclaims Queen Molly, on the Queen Mary, the unanimous winner of the Saddest Sob Story the world has ever known! Molly looking straight at me, gives me a huge smile and blows me a kiss!

Oh, God, Blessed Mother, Grandma, I get it. This is the answer isn't it? This is the answer that has eluded me all these years. Molly's daughter, in order to break her mother's curse once and for all, has to follow in the storytelling tradition of her mother and come up with one huge, whopping lie! A lie she can see and feel! A true Molly lie her daughter can believe and appreciate.

Blessed Mother, *yes*, yes! I can live with this.

Having retrieved the wadded, decades-old scrap of paper and rubbing where I clunked my head, I stand up and move away from the table slowly, very slowly. (Mom, you are so right, slow is definitely my style.) I wave to Ivan as my legs get in gear.

Leaving the bar, I walk out onto the forward deck of the ship. Leaning against the rail, I look over and down into the deep, swirling, fathomless iris of God.

"Our Father, who art in heaven, hallowed be thy name. Thy kingdom come, thy will be done on earth as it is in heaven. Forgive us our trespasses, as we forgive those who trespass against us. Lead us not into temptation but deliver us from evil."

I tear the paper into tiny pieces. A sudden blast of wind snatches the shreds. I'm aware of the gold band of Grandma's twinkling in the deck lights.

Turning from the rail, I hold my own against the strong, wild, wind. I'm back in the sheltered walkway, completely disheveled, but only on the outside; on the inside, I'm feeling pretty good for an old, slow broad.

Walking by the Commodore Bar, I don't need to look in; I see Chuck at the end of the corridor. He sees me. I pick up my pace and he does too. He's carrying my laptop. Earlier, I had thrown it on the bed in disgust before I went back to the Commodore Bar. Both of us stop in the middle of the corridor, and I blurt, "It's over and done. *Nobody's* going to *hell!*"

Whoa! Grabbing me with his free hand, he lifts me off my feet and twirls me around. (He's definitely been working out on this cruise; we've both kept our bargain.)

"I knew you could do it! I've charged your laptop for you."

Putting me back on the ground. I take his face in both hands, kiss him and say, "We really should spend more of Molly's insurance and stamp money on trips; this is fun!"

Chuck squeezes me tightly with his free arm and, with the laptop's light pulsating between us, laughs out loud. He says, "Oh,

Marion, the stories you can tell the grandchildren! I promise I'll back everyone of them up for you."

My story. My truth. Amen.

AUTHOR'S NOTE

The stories of my grandmother and great-grandmother are based on facts, what I heard as a child, my research of birth records, whispered secrets in the family and my imagination as a storyteller. The story of my mother and me, is my own experience and I have told the truth as I know it. As Grandma always said, "God give me strength!"